Meiner Frau Marie-Jeanette voller Dankbarkeit gewidmet.

Widbert Giessing

ISBN: 978-3-9815602-2-0

2. Auflage 2017

Die Veröffentlichung aller Bilder mit Ausnahme der in der
Stadt Potsdam aufgenommenen erfolgt mit freundlicher Genehmigung
der Stiftung Preußische Schlösser und Gärten Berlin-Brandenburg.

www.tertulla.de

Gestaltung: Nadine Hilbrich

Inhalt

Vorwort

In den beeindruckenden Aufnahmen von Widbert Giessing, die Sie in diesem Bildband entdecken werden, spiegelt sich durch ihre artifizielle Wirkung ein Thema wider, das auch uns in der Stiftung Preußische Schlösser und Gärten Berlin-Brandenburg täglich begegnet: das Zusammenspiel von Natur und Kunst. Über Jahrhunderte haben Architekten, Künstler und Gartengestalter im Auftrag ihrer Bauherren, der brandenburgischen Kurfürsten, preußischen Könige und später der deutschen Kaiser, die preußischen Residenzen geschaffen. Die so entstandenen Gesamtkunstwerke zu erforschen, zu erhalten und für die Öffentlichkeit erlebbar zu machen, fordert uns täglich neu. Der Pflegeaufwand und nicht zuletzt die benötigten finanziellen wie personellen Mittel sind enorm. Umso mehr erfreut es meine Mitarbeiter und mich, uns auch bei der Betrachtung dieser brillanten Fotos wieder einmal in unserer Arbeit bestätigt zu sehen und uns daran zu erfreuen. Ich lade Sie herzlich ein, die Originalschauplätze dieser Bilder zu besuchen und dort ihre ganz persönlichen Eindrücke zu gewinnen, in den herrlichen Gärten zu verweilen, und vor Ort zu schauen.

Prof. Dr. Hartmut Dorgerloh

Generaldirektor der Stiftung Preußische Schlösser und Gärten Berlin-Brandenburg

Willkommen in der Brandenburger Landeshauptstadt!
Lassen Sie sich durch die reizvollen Motive und teils ungewöhnlichen Perspektiven verführen, noch mehr zu entdecken: das abwechslungsreiche kulturelle Leben unserer Stadt, ihre Museen, ihre alten und neuen Wahrzeichen. Sie können Potsdam vom Wasser aus erkunden, per Fahrrad oder bei ausgedehnten Spaziergängen. Gestalterische Einflüsse aus vielen Teilen Europas werden Ihnen dabei begegnen: die Russische Kolonie Alexandrowka, das Holländische Viertel, die Französische Kirche, das Böhmische Weberviertel, die Schweizer Häuser in Klein-Glienicke und zahlreiche Turmvillen nach italienischem Vorbild. Sie werden auf Vertrautes, aber auch Ungewohntes treffen, auf historische und moderne Architektur. Das Potsdam von heute ist stolz auf sein geschichtliches Erbe und gestaltet selbstbewusst seine Gegenwart, die stark durch die Wissenschaft und den Film geprägt ist.
Seien Sie uns willkommen in Potsdam!

Jann Jakobs
Oberbürgermeister der Landeshauptstadt Potsdam

Potsdam – der Name dieser Stadt hatte für mich seit jeher einen ganz eigenen Klang und Reiz. Als zwar in Bremen geborener und aufgewachsener Nachfahre jener Kurfürsten, Könige und Kaiser, die hier über Jahrhunderte hindurch residierten, war mir der Ort insbesondere durch die Erzählungen meines Großvaters Prinz Louis Ferdinand von Preußen (1907 – 1994) doch stets vertraut. Er verband als gebürtiger Potsdamer und Enkel Kaiser Wilhelms II. mit dieser Stadt noch Erinnerungen, wie sie heutzutage wohl kaum jemand mehr vermitteln könnte.
Somit empfand auch ich meine ersten Besuche in Potsdam als eine Art Rückkehr und zugleich Neuentdeckung einer mir bis dahin persönlich verschlossen gebliebenen Heimat. Es kam damals zu zahlreichen Begegnungen, aus denen mittlerweile Freundschaften geworden sind. Ich habe mich in Potsdam von Anfang an immer ausgesprochen wohl gefühlt und meine Frau und ich waren uns sofort einig, dass hier auch 2011 unsere Hochzeit stattfinden sollte.
In den letzten Jahrzehnten hat sich in dieser Stadt, in der die Zeit gewissermaßen stehen geblieben und zugleich unerbittlich vorangeschritten war, vieles verändert und erstrahlt inzwischen wieder in neuem Glanz. Dies haben auch die in der vorliegenden Publikation präsentierten HDR-Fotografien auf faszinierende Weise eingefangen, indem sie das aus Architektur und Natur geschaffene „Gesamtkunstwerk Potsdam“ in seiner vielschichtigen Schönheit buchstäblich zum Leuchten bringen.

Georg Friedrich Prinz von Preußen

Preface

In the artificial character of these impressive photographs by Widbert Giessing, which you will discover in this book of images, a topic is reflected that we at the Prussian Palaces and Gardens Foundation of Berlin-Brandenburg encounter daily: The interaction of nature and art. Over the centuries architects, artists and landscape designers created the Prussian residences on behalf of their patrons the Brandenburg electors, Prussian kings and later the German Kaiser. To research, maintain and make experienceable for the public the cumulative work of art that has come about, is a daily challenge for us. The maintenance involved and not least the required financial and human resources are enormous. Thus I and my colleagues are all the more pleased to see our work acknowledged again in these brilliant photos, and are delighted with them. I warmly invite you to visit the original settings of these images and to gain your own personal impression there, to linger in the heavenly gardens and to explore on site.

Prof. Dr. Hartmut Dorgerloh

General Director of the Prussian Palaces and Gardens Foundation Berlin-Brandenburg

Welcome to the Brandenburg capital!
Let yourself be seduced into wanting to discover even more by the beautiful motifs and sometimes unusual perspectives: The diverse cultural life of our city, its museums, and its new and old landmarks. You can discover the city from the water, by bicycle or on extensive strolls. You will encounter creative influences from many parts of Europe: The Russian colony of Alexandrowka, the Dutch quarter, the French church, the Bohemian weavers' quarter, the Swiss houses in Klein-Glienicke and numerous tower villas in Italian style. You will encounter the familiar but also the unusual, historical and modern architecture. Potsdam today is proud of its historical heritage and self-confidently shapes its future, which is strongly influenced by science and film.
We welcome you to Potsdam!

Jann Jakobs
Lord Mayor of the State Capital of Potsdam

Potsdam – for me the name of this city has always had its very own sound and charm. Although I was born and grew up in Bremen, as a descendant of the electors, kings and Kaisers who resided here through the centuries I was always familiar with the area, especially through the stories of my grandfather Prince Louis Ferdinand of Prussia (1907 – 1994). As the Potsdam-born grandson of Kaiser Wilhelm II he still associated memories with this city that these days hardly anyone could impart.
For this reason I felt like my first visit to Potsdam was a kind of return, and at the same time the new discovery of a home which had until that point remained closed to me personally. At that time I had numerous encounters, which in the meantime have become friendships.
I have always, from the very start, felt very comfortable in Potsdam, and my wife and I immediately agreed that our wedding should take place here in 2011.
Over the last decades in this city, where time to some extent has stood still and yet at the same time relentlessly forged ahead, much has changed and nowadays it shines with a new lustre. This has been captured in a fascinating way in the HDR photographs of the present publication, which literally lights up the multi-layered beauty of the „complete artwork of Potsdam", which is created with architecture and nature.

Georg Friedrich Prince of Prussia

Königliches Potsdam

Die Anfänge waren bescheiden. Als Friedrich Wilhelm, der Große Kurfürst, ab Anfang der 1660er Jahre am Potsdamer Havelübergang ein Stadtschloss errichten ließ, war das Stadtbild immer noch durch die Verwüstungen des Dreißigjährigen Kriegs geprägt. 1660 zählte man in Potsdam 198 Hausstellen, davon 119 wüste, also nicht mehr bewohnbare, und lediglich 711 Einwohner. 1664 schrieb der weitgereiste holländische Vertraute des Kurfürsten, Fürst Johann Moritz von Nassau-Siegen, in einem Brief an Friedrich Wilhelm, „das ganze Eiland Potsdam „müsse ein Paradies“ werden – damals reine Zukunftsmusik, kein zu Lebzeiten einlösbares Programm. Doch mit der Anlage zweier vom neuen Schloss aus weit ausgreifender Landschaftsachsen wurden die urbanistischen Entwicklungslinien künftiger Jahrhunderte definiert. Weitblick war die erste Herrscherpflicht.

Potsdam ist ein Kunstprodukt. Vor über 1000 Jahren, im Jahr 993, erstmals urkundlich erwähnt, verdankt die Stadt ihre heutige Bedeutung und Schönheit allein dem Kunstsinn der letzten 350 Jahre. Potsdam wuchs nicht wie andere Städte aufgrund wirtschaftlicher Bedingungen, Potsdam wurde befohlen. Bedeutende Baumeister, Gartengestalter und Künstler haben hier gewirkt, das Bild der Stadt verändert oder diese Wandlung wiederum in Bildern festgehalten. In Zeiten beschränkter Ressourcen war soviel Manpower ein zumal in Nordostdeutschland sehr seltenes Privileg. Die künstlerischen Hinterlassenschaften von Knobelsdorff, Pesne, Schinkel und Lenné faszinieren die Besucher der Stadt bis heute. Sanssouci, das Weinbergschloss, ist zu Recht weltberühmt – ein glückliches Zusammenspiel von Ort, Idee und Realisierung, wie es nicht oft zu finden ist in der Kunstgeschichte.

Potsdam ist die Hohenzollern-Stadt schlechthin. Brandenburgische Kurfürsten und preußische Könige haben Potsdam zwischen 1660 und 1918 so plan- wie absichtsvoll zu ihrer Musterstadt, ihrem Traum- und Rückzugsort, kurz: zu ihrer Lieblingsresidenz gemacht. Herrschernamen wie Friedrich der Große und Friedrich Wilhelm IV. sind untrennbar verbunden mit der Geschichte der Havelstadt, die sich selbst gern als deutsches Versailles sieht. Schlösser wie das Neue Palais wurden auch (oder gerade) in wirtschaftlich schwierigen Zeiten gebaut. Für die Anlage von Gärten und Parks überlistete man die Natur und ließ jahrzehntealte Bäume verpflanzen. Ganze Stadtviertel wurden in den märkischen Sumpf und Sand gestampft und die Bürger – alte wie die aus allen Teilen Europas neu angeworbenen – mit Häusern nach des Königs Geschmack beglückt. Den Potsdamern selbst wird soviel landesherrliche Fürsorge nicht immer gefallen haben. Noch heute spürt man manchmal Ratlosigkeit im Umgang mit „denen da oben", auch wenn sie nicht mehr Friedrich oder Wilhelm, sondern Joop und Jauch heißen.

„Mit den vierzigtausend Einwohnern der guten Stadt Potsdam brauchen wir uns nicht viel zu beschäftigen. Es ist ein harmloses Völkchen, das nicht viel Lärm macht", heißt es 1860 mit spöttischem Unterton in der Unterhaltungsbibliothek für die Leser aller Stände. Die Potsdamer: Das waren Subalterne, keine selbstbewussten Bürger, geschweige denn Revolutionäre. Kein Wunder, dass sich die Nazis am 21. März 1933 Potsdam als Aufführungsort für ihre symbolträchtige Anbiederung ans alte Pickelhauben-Preußen aussuchten. Kein Wunder auch, dass die plebejische DDR wenig mit all dem anzufangen wusste. Ideologisch begründete Abrisse – nicht nur prominenter Ruinen wie des Stadtschlosses und der Garnisonkirche – fügten Potsdam nach Kriegsende mehr Schäden zu als die englischen Bomber, die weite Teile des Stadtzentrums am 14. April 1945 in Schutt und Asche gelegt hatten. Die schleichende Stadtzerstörung durch die sozialistischen Machthaber war einer der Gründe, warum 1989 auch in Potsdam protestiert wurde. Bürgerinitiativen wie ARGUS verhinderten damals in letzter Minute Flächenabrisse in der Zweiten Barocken Stadterweiterung, dem intaktesten Viertel der Innenstadt.

Inzwischen sind nicht nur die erhaltenen Fassaden restauriert und geputzt worden, Potsdam rekonstruiert auch sein Stadtschloss ganz neu aus dem Nichts: als Landtagsgebäude eines irgendwann vielleicht einmal vereinigten Bundeslands Berlin-Brandenburg. Größenwahn und Traditionalismus – auch das gehört zur Potsdamer Mischung. Gleichwohl ist die Stadt mehr als ein begehbares Museum. Die einstige Residenz profiliert sich als lebendige, prosperierende Landeshauptstadt (eine der wenigen Städte Ostdeutschlands mit steigender Einwohnerzahl) und – im Zusammenspiel von Stadtkern und Landschaftsraum – als ein funktionierendes Gesamtkunstwerk. Seit 1990 zählt die Potsdam-Berliner Schlösserlandschaft zum UNESCO-Welterbe. Generationen von Künstlern und Königen haben zum Potsdamer Stadt- und Parkensemble beigetragen. Uns und künftigen Generationen bleibt es vorbehalten, Potsdams einmalige Schönheit, eine Schönheit nach königlichem Plan, zu pflegen und zu erhalten.

Michael Zajonz

Royal Potsdam

The beginnings were modest. When Friedrich Wilhelm, the great elector, had a City Palace built at Potsdam's Havel crossing at the start of the 1660s the cityscape was still shaped by the destruction of the Thirty Years War. In 1660 there were 198 houses in Potsdam, of which 119 were destroyed and no longer inhabitable, and only 711 inhabitants. In 1664 the well-travelled Dutch confidante of the elector, Fürst Johann Moritz von Nassau-Siegen, wrote a letter to Friedrich Wilhelm, saying that „the entire island of Potsdam should become a paradise" – at the time purely dreams of the future, not feasible in his lifetime. However with the laying out of two new palaces on wide ranging grounds the urban development lines of the future centuries were defined. Foresight was the first duty of the rulers.

Potsdam is a work of art. First mentioned over 1000 years ago in a document from 993, the city can thank its modern importance and beauty to the love of art over the past 350 years. Unlike other cities Potsdam did not grow due to economic conditions, Potsdam was designed. Important architects, garden designers and artists worked here, changing the image of the city or capturing these changes in images. In times of limited resources so much manpower was a very seldom privilege in north-east Germany. The artistic legacies of Knobelsdorff, Pesne, Schinkel and Lenné still fascinate visitors to the city today. Sanssouci, the vineyard castle, is rightly world famous – a successful interplay of location, idea and realisation that is seldom found in the history of art.

Potsdam is absolutely the Hohenzollern city. Between 1660 and 1918 Brandenburg electors and Prussian kings planned and deliberately made Potsdam their model city, their dream location and retreat, in short: Their favourite home. Royal names such as Friedrich the Great and Friedrich Wilhelm IV are inseparably linked to the history of the city on the Havel, which likes to see itself as the German Versailles. Palaces such as the New Palace were also built in financially difficult times. For the layout of the gardens and parks nature was outwitted and trees that were decades old were replanted. Whole districts were tamped in the swamp and sand, and the inhabitants – the old ones as well as the newly acquired – were blessed with houses that accorded with the king's tastes. The Potsdamers themselves didn't always like so much sovereign attention. Even today you can sometimes feel the helplessness of dealings with „those up there", even if today they aren't called Friedrich or Wilhelm, but rather Joop and Jauch.

„We don't need to preoccupy ourselves with the forty thousand inhabitants of the city of Potsdam. It is a harmless little crowd that doesn't make much noise" it says with a mocking undertone in an 1860 entertainment library for readers of all levels. The Potsdamers: The true subordinates, not confident citizens, let alone revolutionaries. No wonder that on March 21st, 1933, the Nazis chose Potsdam as the venue for their symbolic ingratiation to the old spiked helmeted Prussians. Also no wonder that the plebeian German Democratic Republic didn't know what to do with it all. Ideologically founded demolition after the end of the war – not only prominent ruins such as the City Palace and the Garrison Church – inflicted more damage than the English bombers that reduced large swathes of the city centre to rubble and ash on April 14th, 1945. The creeping destruction of the city by the socialist rulers was one of the reasons why there were also protests in Potsdam in 1989. At the time citizen initiatives such as ARGUS prevented demolitions of the second baroque city expansion at the last minute, which is now the most intact district of the city centre.

Now not only have the preserved façades been restored and cleaned but Potsdam is reconstructing its City Palace from scratch: As the state parliament building of what might one day be a united state of Berlin-Brandenburg. Megalomania and traditionalism – this is also part of the Potsdam mixture. At the same time the city is more than just an outdoor museum. The former royal residence distinguishes itself as a living, prosperous state capital (one of the few cities in East Germany with an increasing population) and – in the interplay of the city centre and countryside – as a functional synthesis of the arts. Since 1990 the palaces and parks of Potsdam and Berlin have been UNESCO world heritage. Generations of artists and kings have contributed to the Potsdam city and parks. It is up to us and future generations to maintain and preserve Potsdam's former beauty, a beauty that had royal panning as its guidelines.

Michael Zajonz

Schloss Sanssouci

SANS SOUCI

Ein Sommerschloss wollte sich Friedrich II. vor den Toren von Potsdam bauen, einen Ort, wo er ohne Sorgen, „sans souci“, im Kreise befreundeter Künstler und Gelehrter diskutieren und musizieren konnte – ganz so, wie er es in glücklichen Jugendtagen auf Schloss Rheinsberg erlebt hatte. Auf dem „wüsten Berg“, einer Anhöhe westlich der Innenstadt, ließ er ab 1744 sechs Terrassen anlegen, die mit Weinreben und Spalierobst bepflanzt wurden – nur einer von drei Weinbergen, die der überraschend genussfreudige König rund um Potsdam plante.

Auf der obersten Terrasse des Weinbergs, mit weitem Blick auf die umgebende Landschaft, entstand 1745 bis 1747 unter Regie des Architekten Georg Wenzeslaus von Knobelsdorff Friedrichs Sommerschloss Sanssouci. Später kamen zu beiden Seiten noch die Bildergalerie und – durch Umbau der Orangerie zu Gästewohnungen – die Neuen Kammern hinzu.

Erste Ideen für sein Schloss hatte der König selbst gezeichnet, ungewöhnlich bescheiden für eine königliche Residenz: ein ovaler Marmorsaal in der Mitte, dem römischen Pantheon nachgebildet, und zu beiden Seiten ebenerdig jeweils fünf Räume: östlich die Wohnräume des Königs, westlich die Gästezimmer, die sich mit Flügeltüren direkt auf die Terrasse öffnen.

Knobelsdorffs Entwurf, der Skulpturenschmuck von Friedrich Christian Glume mit seinen Anspielungen an Weinbau und Weingenuss und die erlesene Innenausstattung der Gebrüder Hoppenhaupt machen dieses berühmteste Potsdamer Schloss zu einem herausragenden Beispiel des Friderizianischen Rokoko. Hier fanden die Tafelrunden statt, bei denen Friedrich seine Freunde um sich scharte. Drei Jahre, von 1750 bis 1753, war auch der vom König bewunderte französische Philosoph Voltaire zu Gast – ein besonders reich ausgestattetes Zimmer ist nach ihm benannt. Und im Musikzimmer griff der König abends selbst zur Querflöte, begleitet von Carl Philipp Emmanuel Bach und anderen Musikern.

1786 verstarb der König in seinem Arbeitszimmer. 1991 erst wurde er, wie es sein Wunsch gewesen war, in der Gruft auf der obersten Weinbergsterrasse bestattet – neben seinen geliebten Windspielen, die dort über 200 Jahre auf ihren Herren warten mussten.

Sanssouci Palace

Friedrich II wanted to build himself a summer palace at the gates of Potsdam, a place where he could hold discussions and play music without a care, „sans souci", surrounded by artists and scholar friends – just as he had experienced in the happy days of his youth at Rheinsberg palace. On the „desert mountain", a hill to the west of the city centre, in 1744 he had six terraces created which were planted with grape vines and trellised fruit – just one of three vineyards which the epicurean king planted around Potsdam.

On the top terrace of the vineyard, with a marvellous view over the surrounding landscape, Friedrich's summer palace of Sanssouci came into being under the direction of Georg Wenzeslaus von Knobelsdorff between 1745 and 1747. Later, on both sides, there was also the picture gallery and – through conversion of the orangery into a guest apartment – the New Chambers.

The first ideas for his palace were drawn by the king himself and are unusually humble for a king's residence: An oval marble hall in the middle which is modelled on the Pantheon and five rooms on either side: East are the living areas of the king, to the west the guest rooms whose double doors open directly onto the terrace.

Knobelsdorff's design, the adorning sculptures of Friedrich Christian Glume with his allusions to viticulture and enjoyment of wine, and the exquisite interiors from the brothers Hoppenhaupt make this most famous of Potsdam's palaces an outstanding example of the Frederickian rococo. This is where the round tables took place at which Friedrich rallied his friends around himself. For three years, from 1750 to 1753, the French philosopher Voltaire, who the king admired, was a guest here – a particularly richly decorated room is named after him. And in the music room the king himself played the flute, accompanied by Carl Philipp Emmanuel Bach and other musicians.

In 1786 the king died in his study. Only in 1991 was he, as had been his wish, buried in the crypt on the top vineyard terrace – next to his beloved greyhounds, who had had to wait more than 200 years for their master.

◀

Sanssouci, ohne Sorge, nannte Friedrich II. sein Refugium auf dem Weinberg, das neben Privaträumen auch Gästezimmer enthält. Ungewöhnlich war der Verzicht auf ein Sockelgeschoss, um Innen und Außen besser zu verbinden. Die Gebälkträger, Gefolgsleute des Weingottes Bachus, schuf der Bildhauer Friedrich Christian Glume.

Sanssouci, without a care, is what Friedrich II named his vineyard retreat, which also includes guest rooms next to the private rooms. The absence of a basement to better connect the interior and exterior was unusual. The support beams were created by sculptor Friedrich Christian Glume in the form of followers of the wine god Bacchus.

▶

Im östlichen Gitterpavillon (der ein westliches Pendant besitzt) ließ Friedrich vis-à-vis seiner Bibliothek den „Betenden Knaben" aufstellen, eine griechische Großbronze des 4. Jh. v. Chr. 1830 kam das Original in das neugegründete Alte Museum nach Berlin und wurde durch eine Kopie ersetzt.

In the eastern lattice-work pavilion (which has a western counterpart), Friedrich set up the „Praying Boy" statue, a large Greek bronze from the 4th century BC, opposite his library. In 1830 the original was moved to the newly established Altes Museum in Berlin and a reproduction took its place.

▶
Die Verbindung von Schloss und Garten findet im 1744 angelegten Weinberg ihren Höhepunkt. In verglasten Nischen und an Spalieren wurden Trauben und Tafelobst gezogen.

The connection of the palace and garden reached its peak in 1744 when the landscaped vineyard was established. Fruit and table grapes were drawn on glazed alcoves and trellises.

▶▶
Überall im Park finden sich Skulpturen aus kostbarem Carrara-Marmor. Auf der obersten Schlossterrasse ließ Friedrich nicht nur seine Windhunde begraben, sondern auch für sich selbst eine Gruft anlegen.

Sculptures in precious Carrara marble can be found all over the park. On the palace's upper terrace, Friedrich not only had his greyhounds buried, but also created a tomb for himself.

▶▶▶
Der von einer halbrunden Säulenkolonnade umgrenzte Ehrenhof – eigentlich der Haupteingang des Schlosses – lenkt den Blick auf den Ruinenberg, eine künstliche Ruinenstaffage, die ein Wasserreservoir kaschiert.

The courtyard, bounded by a semicircular colonnade – actually the main entrance to the palace – draws the eye to the mountain of ruins, an artificial ruin that conceals a water reservoir.

◀
Das Motiv der gekuppelten Säulen entlehnte Georg Wenzeslaus von Knobelsdorff, der Architekt von Schloss Sanssouci, der berühmten Ostfassade des Pariser Louvre.

Georg Wenzeslaus von Knobelsdorff, architect of Sanssouci Palace, borrowed the double-column motif from the famous east façade of the Louvre in Paris.

▶
Östlich und westlich des Weinbergs rahmen Schloss Sanssouci äußerlich ähnliche Nebengebäude. Im Westen des Schlosses stehen die Neuen Kammern, ursprünglich als Orangerie errichtet und in den 1770er Jahren durch Georg Christian Unger zum Gästehaus mit komfortablen Appartements und Festsälen umgebaut. Eine Umgestaltung der Rückseite des Gebäudes, hier im Bild, erfolgte Mitte des 19. Jahrhunderts durch Ludwig Persius.

East and west of the vineyard, externally similar outbuildings frame Sanssouci Palace. The New Chambers are to be found to the west of the palace. Originally built as an orangery, the chambers were rebuilt as a guest house in the 1770s by Georg Christian Unger, offering comfortable apartments and banqueting halls. A redesign of the rear of the building, pictured here, was carried out in the mid-19th century by Ludwig Persius.

◀
Östlich von Schloss Sanssouci ließ Friedrich II. durch Johann Gottfried Büring die Bildergalerie errichten: heute der älteste fürstliche Museumsbau in Deutschland. Die lange Bauzeit von 1755 bis 1764 erklärt sich durch den Siebenjährigen Krieg. Neben französischen Rokoko-Gemälden von Antoine Watteau und anderen sammelte Friedrich italienische und flämische Meister des 16. und 17. Jahrhunderts.

To the east of Sanssouci Palace, Friedrich II commissioned Johann Gottfried Büring to build the Picture Gallery, the oldest royal museum in Germany today. The long construction period from 1755 to 1764 is explained by the Seven Years' War. Alongside French Rococo paintings by Antoine Watteau and others, Friedrich collected paintings by Italian and Flemish masters of the 16th and 17th centuries.

▶
Der Skulpturenschmuck der Bildergalerie – neben Vasen auch Allegorien auf Künste und Wissenschaften – stammt von den Potsdamer Bildhauern Johann Gottlieb Heymüller und Johann Peter Benkert.

The Picture Gallery sculptures, besides vases allegories for the arts and sciences, were created by Potsdam sculptors Johann Gottlieb Heymüller and Johann Peter Benkert.

Im Park Sanssouci

Montag bis Freitag
von 7.00-17.00 Uhr
Einfahrt über den Schirrhof
Lennéstraße 10

Sie haben es in ihren Stadtschlössern nicht lange ausgehalten, Preußens Könige – und sich dafür im Verlauf von zwei Jahrhunderten ein einzigartiges Gartenreich geschaffen. Vor den Toren Potsdams erblühten Träume von Italien und fernen Ländern, wuchsen Tempelchen, französische, englische, italienische Gartenanlagen, Gewächshäuser, Landvillen und Aussichtstürme aus dem märkischen Sand.

Friedrich II. hatte den Anfang gemacht mit seinem Weinbergschloss Sanssouci, von dessen Terrasse aus er über Rondelle und Bukette, Wasserbecken und Alleen blickte. Der „alte Fritz" ließ Weinberge anlegen und Obstplantagen, wollte so früh wie möglich im Jahr mit Kirschen, Birnen, Pflaumen, Aprikosen und Trauben versorgt werden, ließ Melonen und Ananas in Treibhäusern ziehen: Träume vom Süden im kalten Norden, für die der sparsame König viel Geld investierte. Auch seine Parklandschaft gestaltete er nach barockem Vorbild. Gemäß der damaligen Mode baute er sich ein chinesisches Teehaus in den Park und ein ebenfalls chinesisch inspiriertes Drachenhaus auf dem Klausberg, in dem der Winzer wohnte. Heute ist dort, unweit des nach 1989 rekonstruierten Belvederes, ein Café.

Besonders König Friedrich Wilhelm IV., der „Romantiker auf dem Thron", baute fleißig weiter am Gartentraum von Sanssouci. Der klassizistisch-romantische Zeitgeist des frühen 19. Jahrhunderts verlangte nach Ruhebänken an schattigen Plätzen, Grotten und Pergolen, Statuen und Hermen, nach aus dem Boden sprudelnden Fontänen, Kanälen, Brücken und weiten Sichtachsen. Der große Gartengestalter Peter Joseph Lenné hat mit der Umgestaltung und Erweiterung des südlichen Schlossparks ein Meisterstück vollbracht und Gesamtkunstwerke wie den Marlygarten oder den Sizilianischen Garten geschaffen. In der zur Stadt Potsdam hin gelegenen Friedenskirche, einer italienischen Basilika nachempfunden, fand der tiefreligiöse König mit seiner Frau Elisabeth von Bayern die letzte Ruhe, ebenso Kaiser Friedrich III. mit seiner englischen Frau Victoria.

Sanssouci Park

The Prussian kings didn't last long in their city palaces – and for that reason they created a unique garden kingdom over the course of two hundred years. At the gates of Potsdam, dreams of Italy and foreign countries blossomed, and little temples, French, English and Italian gardens, greenhouses, country villas and lookout towers grew out of the sand.

Friedrich II made a start with his vineyard palace Sanssouci, from whose terrace he could look out over turrets and bouquets of flowers, pools and avenues. The „old Fritz" had vineyards and orchards planted, and wanted to be provided with cherries, pears, plums, apricots and grapes as early in the year as possible, he also had melons and pineapples grown in greenhouses: Dreams of the south in the cold north, for which the frugal king invested a lot of money. He also created his park landscape based on a Baroque model. In accordance with the fashion at the time he built himself a Chinese tea house in the park and an equally Chinese inspired dragon house on Klausberg hill, in which the winemakers lived. Today there is a café in it, not far from post 1989 reconstruction of Belvedere.

In particular King Friedrich Wilhelm IV, the „romantic on the throne", industriously continued building the garden dream of Sanssouci. The classical romantic zeitgeist of the early 19th century required relaxation benches in shady corners, grottos and pergolas, statues and herms, fountains that bubbled out of the ground, canals, bridges and wide vistas. The great garden designer Peter Joseph Lenné accomplished a masterpiece with his transformation and expansion of the southern palace landscape, and created complete works of art such as the Marly Garden or the Sicilian Garden. In the Church of Peace located in Potsdam, a recreation of an Italian basilica, the deeply religious king was laid to rest with his wife Elisabeth von Bayern, as was Kaiser Friedrich III with his English wife Victoria.

▶
Das Obeliskportal markiert als östlicher Haupteingang zum Schlosspark den Beginn der 2,5 Kilometer langen, in Ost-West-Richtung verlaufenden Hauptallee. In ihrer Sichtweite liegen viele Parkbauten wie die Perlen einer Kette aufgereiht. Als Fixpunkt lockt die Kuppel des Neuen Palais.

The Obelisk portal as eastern main entrance to the park marks the beginning of the 2.5 km long main avenue, which runs from east to west. Within eyesight of the avenue, numerous architectural features are strung along it like pearls on a string. The dome of the New Palace stands as a fixed landmark.

▶▶
Erster gartenkünstlerischer Höhepunkt an der Hauptallee ist das Oranierrondell vor der Bildergalerie. Benannt wurde es nach Marmorbüsten der holländischen Verwandtschaft des Hauses Hohenzollern. Im 17. Jahrhundert waren die dynastischen Bindungen zwischen Brandenburg-Preußen und den Niederlanden besonders eng.

The first horticultural highlight on the main avenue is the Orange Roundel in front of the Picture Gallery. It was named after the marble busts of members of the Dutch relatives of the House of Hohenzollern. In the 17th century the dynastic ties between Brandenburg-Prussia and the Netherlands were particularly close.

Nur wenige Meter abseits der Hauptallee erhebt sich die malerische Baugruppe der Friedenskirche am Ufer eines künstlichen Teichs. König Friedrich Wilhelm IV., bekannt als „Romantiker auf dem Thron", träumte Mitte des 19. Jahrhunderts von der Wiederbelebung urchristlicher Traditionen. Die Friedenskirche mit der Gruft des Königs und seiner Gemahlin Elisabeth von Bayern vereinigt die Gestalt einer frühchristlichen römischen Basilika mit Motiven des deutschen Mittelalters.

Just a few metres away from the main avenue stands the picturesque assembly of Friedenskirche buildings on the banks of an artificial pond. During the mid-19th century, King Friedrich Wilhelm IV, known as the "romantic on the throne", dreamed of a revival of early Christian traditions. The Friedenskirche, containing the tomb of the king and his wife Elisabeth von Bayern, combines the design of an early Roman Christian basilica with features from the German Middle Ages.

Wie ein Freiluftmuseum der Bildhauerkunst mutet der Schlosspark an. Friedrich II. ließ am Hauptrondell vor den Weinbergsterrassen Skulpturen antiker Götter aufstellen, geschaffen zumeist von französischen Bildhauern (S. 38). Für die Grazie und Eleganz des Rokoko stehen Venus und Merkur, zwei Meisterwerke von Jean-Baptiste Pigalle (S. 39). Im 19. Jahrhundert wurde der Skulpturenschmuck in Sichtweite des Schlosses weiter ergänzt, etwa durch Figurengruppen mit klassizistischen Marmorwannen.

The park is like an open-air museum of sculpture. Friedrich II placed sculptures of ancient gods at the main roundel in front of the vineyard terraces, created mostly by French sculptors (p. 38). Venus and Mercury, two masterpieces by Jean-Baptiste Pigalle (p. 39), stand for the grace and elegance of the Rococo period. In the 19th century the sculptures in sight of the palace were added to, for example with groups of figures and classical marble baths.

Auch die Architektur im Park bietet romantische Motive. Berühmt ist die Mühle von Sanssouci. Ihr Klappern soll, so die – nicht wahrheitsgemäße – Legende, König Friedrich im nahen Schloss Sanssouci gestört haben. Unweit der Mühle liegt der Sizilianische Garten, eine Schöpfung des Gartengestalters Peter Joseph Lenné, mit seiner prächtigen Gartenmauer.

The park's architecture also offers romantic motifs. Sanssouci's Historic Mill is famous. Its rattling, so the apocryphal legend goes, disturbed King Friedrich in the nearby palace. Not far from the mill lies the Sicilian Garden, creation of landscape designer Peter Joseph Lenné, complete with its magnificent garden wall.

Das Chinesische (Tee-)Haus von Sanssouci ist bei Besuchern besonders beliebt. Errichtet nach Skizzen von Friedrich II. durch Johann Gottfried Büring, spiegelt es die höfische Chinamode des 18. Jahrhunderts wieder. Die Gruppen musizierender und Tee trinkender Chinesen aus vergoldetem Sandstein schufen Johann Gottlieb Heymüller und Johann Peter Benkert. In unmittelbarer Nähe hat sich auch das zugehörige Küchengebäude erhalten.

The Sanssouci Chinese (Tea) House is very popular with visitors. Built by Johann Gottfried Büring according to Friedrich II's sketches, it reflects the courtly fashion for all Chinese things in the 18th century. The gilt sandstone groups of Chinese making music and drinking tea were created by Johann Gottlieb Heymüller and Johann Peter Benkert. Next door the associated kitchen building has also been preserved.

Auch jenseits ausgetretener Hauptwege lassen sich im Schlosspark überall erstaunliche Entdeckungen machen. Dazu gehört das Drachenhaus, 1770 von Carl von Gontard im Stil einer chinesischen Pagode entworfen. Friedrich II. ließ das pittoreske Parkgebäude dem Vorbild einer wesentlich größeren Pagode von Sir William Chambers im englischen Landschaftspark Kew Gardens nachempfinden.

There are also amazing discoveries to be made off the beaten track in the park. These include the Dragon House, designed by Carl von Gontard in 1770 in the style of a Chinese pagoda. Friedrich II requested that this picturesque park building was modelled on a much larger pagoda by Sir Wilhelm Chambers in the English Kew Gardens.

Wenige Schritte vom Drachenhaus entfernt strahlt das Belvedere auf dem Klausberg heute wieder im alten Glanz. Noch 1990 bot das von 1770 bis 1772 von Georg Christian Unger nach antik-römischem Vorbild errichtete Aussichtsbauwerk einen traurigen Anblick. Artilleriebeschuss während der letzten Kriegstage 1945 und jahrzehntelange Vernachlässigung hatten aus der eleganten Säulenarchitektur eine Ruine werden lassen. Mit Mitteln der Münchner Messerschmitt Stiftung gelang der denkmalgerechte Wiederaufbau des Außenbaus und der kostbaren Innenräume.

A few steps away from the Dragon House, the Belvedere on the Klausberg has today been restored to its former glory. In 1990, the model of an ancient Roman building, built in 1770-72 by Georg Christian Unger, was a sorry sight. Artillery fire during the last days of the war in 1945, added to decades of neglect, had turned the elegant columns of this building into a ruin. With the help of the Munich Messerschmitt Foundation, a historically appropriate reconstruction of the exterior and precious interior of this building was achieved.

Am westlichen Ende der Hauptallee erhebt sich das Neue Palais, das zweite Schloss im Park Sanssouci aus friderizianischer Zeit. Ihm vorgelagert im Rehgarten, einem eher naturbelassenen Parkteil, finden sich barocke Parkarchitekturen wie der filigrane Gartenpavillon aus geschmiedetem Gitterwerk. Ein besonderes Kleinod ist auch der Freundschaftstempel aus grauweißem Marmor, den Friedrich der Große der besonders engen Beziehung zu seiner Lieblingsschwester Wilhelmine Markgräfin von Bayreuth gewidmet hat.

At the western end of the main avenue rises the New Palace, the second palace in Sanssouci Park from Friedrich's time. In front of it lies the deer park, a more natural part of the park, where you will find baroque constructions such as the sophisticated gazebo of forged latticework. Another particular gem is the grey-white marble Temple of Friendship, which Friedrich the Great dedicated to his particularly close relationship with his favourite sister, Wilhelmine, Margravine of Bayreuth.

Neues Palais

Er wollte noch einmal ein richtig großes Schloss bauen, auch wenn Preußen nach dem Siebenjährigen Krieg finanziell am Ende war. Fanfaronade, Prahlerei, hat Friedrich II. seinen Schlossplan genannt – eine Arbeitsbeschaffungsmaßnahme für das kriegsgebeutelte Land. Der 1763 bis 1769 von Johann Gottfried Büring, Heinrich Ludwig Manger und dem aus Bayreuth stammenden Carl von Gontard entworfene Bau ist eine weitläufige Barockanlage mit Ehrenhof und Eckpavillons. Das Neue Palais steht am westlichen Ende der den Park teilenden Hauptallee. Selbst seine Wirtschaftsgebäude, Communs genannt, sind mit Kuppeln, Freitreppen und Säulen geschmückt. Heute sitzt hier die Universität Potsdam mit Instituten.

Gewohnt hat Friedrich II. eher selten im neuen Schloss. Bis zu seinem Tod zog er sein intimes Privatdomizil Sanssouci auf dem Weinberg vor. Sein Quartier im Neuen Palais mit Musikzimmer, Bibliothek und Arbeitskabinetten lag wenig repräsentativ im südlichen Eckpavillon. Im benachbarten barocken Schlosstheater, das bis heute bespielt wird, ließ Friedrich italienische Opern und französische Dramen aufführen.

Potsdams größtes Schloss war zugleich sein unbelebtestes. Die 300 Zimmer des Neuen Palais wurden als Gästewohnungen nach Friedrichs Tod nur noch sporadisch genutzt – so altmodisch unbequem war ihr Standard. Erst nach 1859 zog wieder Leben ins Schloss: Friedrich III., der 99-Tage-Kaiser, erwählte es zu seinem Sommersitz und nannte es „Friedrichskron“. 1888 starb er hier. Auch sein Sohn Wilhelm II. nutzte das Schloss, das er umfassend modernisierte: mit Bädern, Wasserklosetts, Zentralheizung, Elektrizität und Fahrstuhl.

Heute ist das prachtvolle Gebäude mit seinen Appartements, der Marmorgalerie und dem Grottensaal ein Sorgenkind der Stiftung Preußische Schlösser und Gärten. Die Sanierung des gewaltigen Baus wird trotz großer Fortschritte wohl noch Jahre in Anspruch nehmen.

He wanted to once more build a massive palace, even if the Prussians were financially ruined after the Seven Years War. Friedrich II named his palace plan fanfaronade, vainglory – a job creation scheme for the war-torn country. The construction, which was created between 1763 and 1769 by Johann Gottfried Büring, Heinrich Ludwig Manger and Carl von Gontard from Bayreuth, is an extensive Baroque complex with courtyards and corner pavilions. The New Palace is at the western end of the main axial avenue which divides the park. Even its working quarters, called the Communs, are adorned with domes, staircases and pillars. Today they are used by the University of Potsdam.

Friedrich II only seldom lived in his New Palace. Up to his death he preferred his intimate private residence of Sanssouci above the vineyards. His quarters in the New Palace, with music room, library and working cabinets are not very prestigiously located in the southern corner pavilion. In the neighbouring Baroque palace theatre, that is still used today, Friedrich had Italian operas and French dramas performed.

Potsdam's largest palace was at the same time its most lifeless. The 300 rooms of the New Palace were only sporadically used as guest quarters after Friedrich's death – their condition was so old-fashioned and uncomfortable. Only after 1859 did new life come to the palace: Friedrich III, the 99 day Kaiser, selected it as his summer residence and called it „Friedrichskron". In 1888 he died here. His son Wilhelm II also used the palace and comprehensively updated it: With bathrooms, water closets, central heating, electricity and a lift.

Today the magnificent building with its apartments, the marble gallery and the grotto hall is a problem child for the Prussian Palaces and Gardens Foundation. The renovation of the massive building will probably take many more years despite great progress.

Friedrich selbst nannte das unmittelbar nach dem Siebenjährigen Krieg von 1763 bis 1769 gebaute Neue Palais eine „Fanfaronade", eine Prahlerei. Mit dem kostspieligen Neubau wollte der König beweisen, dass Preußen auch ökonomisch siegreich geblieben war. Neben Festsälen, einem Theater und fürstlichen Gästeappartements enthielt das weitläufige Gebäude – im eingeschossigen südlichen Seitenflügel – einige Wohnräume für den König. Als Sommerresidenz bewohnt und maßvoll modernisiert wurde das Neue Palais noch einmal zwischen 1888 und 1918 durch die beiden letzten deutschen Kaiser Friedrich III. und Wilhelm II.

Friedrich himself admitted that the New Palace, built from 1763-69 immediately after the end of the Seven Years' War, was a „fanfaronade", or showing off. With this costly construction, the king wanted to prove that Prussia had also remained economically victorious. In addition to banqueting halls, a theatre and princely guest apartments, the extensive building contained living quarters for the king in the single-storey south wing. Used as a summer residence, the New Palace was extensively modernised from 1888-1918 by the last two German Kaisers, Friedrich III and Wilhelm II.

◀
Was als Gartenterrasse des Neuen Palais wie schönstes Friderizianisches Rokoko wirkt, entstand tatsächlich erst als Zutat unter Kaiser Wilhelm II. um 1900.

The garden terrace of the New Palace, which appears to be a beautiful example of Frederician Rococo, actually came into being under Kaiser Wilhelm II around 1900.

◀◀
Wie eine barocke Theaterkulisse erstreckt sich jenseits des Schlosshofs die bewegte Baugruppe der Communs. Jean Laurent Legeay und Carl von Gontard konzipierten die Communs nicht nur als prächtige Hülle für Neben- und Wirtschaftsräume, sondern auch als eine Art architektonisches Gegenmodell zum Neuen Palais. Anregungen fanden sie in niederländischen und englischen Vorbildern.

Like a baroque theatre set, the Communs group of buildings extends beyond the palace court-yard. Jean Laurent Legeay and Carl von Gontard designed the Communs not only as a superb cover for the ancillary and commercial areas, but also as a kind of architectural counter-model to the New Palace. They took inspiration from Dutch and English models.

Charlottenhof, Römische Bäder und Orangerie

Sie wollten bürgerlich wohnen, nicht residieren: Kronprinz Friedrich Wilhelm, der spätere Friedrich Wilhelm IV., und seine Frau Elisabeth von Bayern. Am südlichen Rand des Parks von Sanssouci entwarf Karl Friedrich Schinkel 1826 für sie das Idealbild eines klassizistischen Landhauses, das der sentimentale Kronprinz „Siam" nannte, Land der Freien. Das zweigeschossige Gebäude, das nur zehn bescheidene Wohnräume umfasst und sich mit einem Säulenportikus auf die Terrasse öffnet, bildet mit seinen Ausblicken in das umgebende Gartenreich von Peter Joseph Lenné eine gelungene Synthese zwischen Natur, Architektur und Kunst. Charlottenhof ist Preußens intimstes, menschlichstes Königsschloss.

Der kronprinzliche Antikentraum von Charlottenhof hat sein bäuerliches Pendant bekommen, nur wenige Meter entfernt. 1829 bis 1840 erbaute Ludwig Persius nach Plänen von Schinkel und Friedrich Wilhelm IV. mit den Römischen Bädern die romantische Fantasie des als italienische Villa getarnten Hofgärtnerhauses samt rekonstruierter römischer Badanlage. Pergolen, Arkaden, Lauben und Gärten umgeben den reizvollen Gebäudekomplex, der sich an toskanischen Landhäusern des 15. Jahrhunderts orientiert. Die Idee der italienischen Villa war Vorbild für diversen Bauten, die Persius und andere im Potsdamer Stadtraum verwirklichten.

Seine Italienleidenschaft krönte Friedrich Wilhelm IV. mit der Großen Orangerie auf der Höhe am Nordrand des Parks. Die Monumentalarchitektur, die 1851 bis 1864 nach Vorgaben des architekturbegeisterten Königs entstand, ist eine Mischung aus Villa Medici und Uffizien. Zwei 90 Meter lange Pflanzenhallen rahmen den Raffaelsaal mit fast 50 Kopien des bewunderten italienischen Malers. Bekrönt wird das Orangerieschloss von Belvedere-Türmen mit verbindender Kolonnade. Insgesamt ist die Orangerie, die heute noch zur Winterlagerung der exotischen Kübelpflanzen genutzt wird, eine einzigartige Architekturfantasie. Der Journalist Victor Auburtin nannte sie 1911 eine „kolossale Zwecklosigkeit."

Charlottenhof, Roman Baths and the Orangery

They wanted to live like civilians, not reside: Crown prince Friedrich Wilhelm, later Friedrich Wilhelm IV and his wife Elisabeth von Bayern. In 1826 on the southern edge of Sanssouci's park, Karl Friedrich Schinkel created the ideal of a classical country house for them, which the sentimental crown prince called „Siam", the land of the free. The two-story building that only has ten modest living rooms and opens onto the terrace with a pillared portico, forms a successful synthesis between nature, architecture and art with its views into the surrounding gardens of Peter Joseph Lenné. Charlottenhof is Prussia's most intimate and human king's palace.

The crown prince's dream of antiquity in Charlottenhof received its counterpart only a few meters away. With the building of the Roman baths from 1829 to 1840 according to plans by Schinkel and Friedrich Wilhelm IV, Ludwig Persius built the romantic fantasy with a lodge for the court gardener which was disguised as an Italian villa, including a reconstructed Roman bathing area. Pergolas, arcades, arbours and gardens surround the attractive complex of buildings, which follow the model of Tuscan style country houses of the 15th century. The idea of the Italian villa was the model for various buildings which Persius and others built in the Potsdam city area.

Friedrich Wilhelm IV crowned his passion for Italy with the large orangery on the hill at the northern edge of the park. The monumental architecture, which came into being between 1851 and 1864 based on guidelines of the king who was an architecture enthusiast, is a combination of Villa Medici and Uffizi. Two 90 meter long halls of plants frame the Raffael Hall, which has almost 50 copies of the admired Italian painter. The orangery palace is crowned with Belvedere towers with connecting colonnades. Overall the orangery, which is today used for winter storage of the exotic potted plants, is a unique architectural fantasy. In 1911 the journalist Victor Auburtin called it „colossal uselessness".

Charlottenhof, für den Kronprinzen und späteren König Friedrich Wilhelm IV. von 1826 bis 1829 nach Entwürfen Karl Friedrich Schinkels aus einem barocken Gutshaus umgebaut, ist mehr ein Landhaus als ein Schloss – und eines der schönsten Raumensembles des frühen 19. Jahrhunderts. Mustergültig verkörpern die klassizistisch-biedermeierlichen Innenräume den sparsamen Geist der neuen Zeit. Der durch Pergola, Rundbank (Exedra) und Wasserbecken raumgreifende Hausgarten wurde um 1910 zum Wallfahrtsort junger Architekten, die später berühmt werden sollten: Walter Gropius, Ludwig Mies van der Rohe, Le Corbusier.

Charlottenhof Palace, rebuilt by Karl Friedrich Schinkel from 1826-29 as a baroque manor house for the Crown Prince and later King Friedrich Wilhelm IV, is more of a country house than a palace, and also one of the most beautiful collections of rooms from the early 19th century. The classic Biedermeier interiors embody the economical spirit of the new age. The spacious garden, with its pergola, circular bench (exedra) and ponds, became a place of pilgrimage around 1910 for young architects who would later become famous: Walter Gropius, Ludwig Mies van der Rohe, Le Corbusier.

In unmittelbarer Verlängerung des Hausgartens schuf der bedeutende Gartenkünstler Peter Joseph Lenné mit dem Rosengarten eine geometrische Gartenachse, die sich an Vorbildern der italienischen Renaissance orientiert. Durch die kleinteilige Gestaltung mit Teppichbeeten und Hecken gestaltete Lenné einen Gartenbereich, der die intimen Innenräume des Schlosses nach außen spiegelt. Sparsam werden Blickpunkte im Garten durch Skulpturen akzentuiert – hier sind es Apollino und Klio, Bronzekopien nach antiken Originalen.

As an immediate extension of the Charlottenhof garden, well-known landscape designer Peter Joseph Lenné created a geometric garden axis with the Rose Garden, based on ideas from the Italian Renaissance. Through the small-scale design using carpet shrubs and hedges, Lenné designed a garden which outwardly reflected the intimate interiors of the palace. Points of view in the garden are economically accented using sculptures - here you will find Apollino and Clio, bronze reproductions of ancient originals.

Unweit von Schloss Charlottenhof erhebt sich am Ufer des künstlich angelegten Maschinenteichs die Baugruppe der Römischen Bäder. Sie entstand ab 1829 als Gemeinschaftswerk von Kronprinz Friedrich Wilhelm, Karl Friedrich Schinkel und dessen Schüler Ludwig Persius. Angestrebt war die getreue Nachahmung von Innenräumen römischer Thermen und Villen, wie sie in Pompeji und Herculaneum ausgegraben worden waren und die romantische Phantasie des Bauherrn anregten. Die äußere Gestalt bestimmen das im italienischen Landhausstil errichtete Gärtnerhaus und der klassizistische Teepavillon.

Not far from the Charlottenhof Palace, the architecture of the Roman Baths lies on the banks of an artificial pond. It was created in 1829 as a joint project by the Crown Prince Friedrich Wilhelm, Karl Friedrich Schinkel and his student Ludwig Persius. The aim was a faithful reproduction of the interior of Roman baths and villas as they had been unearthed at Pompeii and Herculaneum, and which had awakened the romantic imagination of the owner. The outer design is characterised by the Italian rustic style garden house and the neo-classical tea pavilion.

Peter Joseph Lenné, der große preußische Gartenkünstler des 19. Jahrhunderts, schuf mit dem Parkteil Charlottenhof sein Meisterstück. Nirgendwo sonst in der Berlin-Potsdamer Kulturlandschaft verbinden sich Architektur, gestaltete Natur und bildende Kunst so zwanglos und feinsinnig. Im turmbewehrten Hofgärtnerhaus lebte Ludwig Hermann Sello, der bedeutendste Vertreter einer in Potsdam tätigen Gärtnerdynastie. Dort gab es auch Zimmer für die Gäste des Kronprinzenpaars, etwa für Alexander von Humboldt.

Peter Joseph Lenné, the great Prussian landscape designer of the 19th century, created his masterpiece in the Charlottenhof park. Nowhere else in the Berlin-Potsdam cultural landscape are architecture, landscaped nature and fine art so freely and subtly combined. The turreted garden house was home to Ludwig Hermann Sello, the most important representative of a gardening dynasty based in Potsdam. There was also room for the guests of the Crown Prince and his wife, such as Alexander von Humboldt.

Die Neue Orangerie von Sanssouci, auch Orangerieschloss genannt, weil in ihrem Mittelteil der Raffaelsaal mit Kopien von Gemälden des italienischen Renaissancemeisters sowie zwei fürstliche Appartements untergebracht sind, ist ebenfalls eine Schöpfung Friedrich Wilhelms IV. Auf dem Bornstedter Höhenzug am Nordrand des Parks plante der König eine Triumphstraße aus monumentalen Gebäuden, Viadukten, Terrassen und Gartenanlagen. Die Orangerie, von 1851 bis 1864 nach seinen Ideen von Friedrich August Stüler und Ludwig Ferdinand Hesse ausgeführt, gehört zu den wenigen verwirklichten Teilen des Großprojekts.

The Sanssouci New Orangery is also known as the Orangery Palace because its middle section is broken up by the Raffael Hall, complete with reproductions of paintings by the Italian Renaissance master, and two royal suites. It is also a creation of Friedrich Wilhelm IV. On the Bornstedt hill at the northern edge of the park, the king planned a triumphal street with monumental buildings, viaducts, terraces and gardens. The Orangery, built from 1851 to 1864 by Friedrich August Stüler and Ludwig Ferdinand Hesse according to his ideas, is one of the few parts of this ambitious project that were realised.

◀
Auf der Balustrade der oberen Terrasse steht ein Bronzeabguss der „Kranzwerfenden Viktoria" von Christian Daniel Rauch.

A bronze cast of „Victoria throwing the Crown" by Christian Daniel Rauch sits on the balustrade of the upper terrace.

Südliches Flair in der Mark Brandenburg: Der über 300 Meter lange Baukörper der Orangerie erinnert auf Wunsch des italophilen Königs an florentinische Vorbilder der Renaissance wie die Villa Medici oder die Uffizien. Das Standbild Friedrich Wilhelms IV. von Gustav Bläser wurde erst 1873 in der Hauptachse des Mittelbaus aufgestellt.

Southern flair in Brandenburg: at the request of the italophile King, the Orangery building, stretching for over 300 metres, echoes classics of the Florentine Renaissance such as the Villa Medici and the Uffizi. The statue of Friedrich Wilhelm IV by Gustav Bläser was first placed in the main axis of the central building in 1873.

◀
Ein Hauch von Schwermut umweht die Orangerie – wie viele der späten Bauprojekte des politisch glücklosen Königs. Friedrich Wilhelm IV. starb am 2. Januar 1861 im nahen Schloss Sanssouci, ohne die Fertigstellung der Orangerie erlebt zu haben.

The Orangery exudes a touch of melancholy, as do many of the later construction projects of the politically hapless king. Friedrich Wilhelm IV died on 2nd January 1861 in the nearby Sanssouci Palace, without living to see the Orangery completed.

▶
Zum 25. Jubiläum seiner Thronbesteigung im Jahre 1913 ließ Kaiser Wilhelm II. unterhalb der Orangerie eine weitere Gartenterrasse hinzufügen. Ästhetisch steht die Jubiläumsterrasse ganz in der Tradition des 19. Jahrhunderts.

To celebrate the 25th anniversary of his accession to the throne in 1913, Kaiser Wilhelm II added a further garden terrace below the Orangery. The anniversary terrace is completely in the tradition of the 19th century.

Rund um den Neuen Garten

Séancen sollen hier stattgefunden haben und Treffen eines Geheimbunds. Friedrich Wilhelm II., der seinem kinderlosen Onkel Friedrich II. auf dem Thron folgte, schuf sich am Heiligen See eine Art Gegen-Sanssouci. Auch hier Weinberge und Gartenkunst, auch hier ein Schloss, das erlesen nach dem Geschmack der Zeit ausgestattet war. Doch wo in Sanssouci an Friedrichs Tafelrunde der Geist der Aufklärung wehte, umgab sich sein Neffe mit Freimaurern und Mitgliedern des Rosenkreuzerordens und wandelte allein sinnend durch den Park.

Das Marmorpalais, das ihm Carl von Gontard an das Ufer des Heiligen Sees baute, ist von Carl Gotthard Langhans mit schönsten frühklassizistischen Innenräumen ausgestattet worden. Mindestens so reizvoll ist der es umgebende Neue Garten, angelegt in Form eines romantischen Landschaftsparks. Da versinkt eine korinthische Tempelruine am Seeufer halb im Boden – das Gebäude beherbergt die Schlossküche und ist mit diesem durch einen unterirdischen Gang verbunden. Ein Eiskeller in der Form einer Pyramide soll den Zugang zur Unterwelt symbolisieren. Eine Muschelgrotte diente der Zusammenkunft der Logenbrüder. In der Meierei wurde die Milch der im Park weidenden Kühe verarbeitet, im Palmensaal der Orangerie gab und gibt es heute noch Konzerte. Und am südlichen Ende des Parks beherbergte die turmartige Gotische Bibliothek mehr als 1000 Bücher.

Nach dem Tod Friedrich Wilhelms II. geriet der Weiterbau des Marmorpalais ins Stocken und wurde erst von Friedrich Wilhelm IV. vollendet, der auf dem benachbarten Pfingstberg gleich noch ein pompöses Belvedere errichten ließ. Neues Leben kam mit Kronprinz Wilhelm in den Neuen Garten. Der Sohn Kaiser Wilhelms II. lebte ab 1905 mit seiner Gemahlin Cecilie im Marmorpalais, bis 1917 der benachbarte Cecilienhof fertiggestellt war. Hier, im letzten Hohenzollernschloss, das Paul Schultze-Naumburg dem anglophilen Kronprinzenpaar in Form eines englischen Landhauses entwarf, wohnte die Familie bis zum Ende des Zweiten Weltkriegs. Kurz danach, vom 17. Juli bis zum 2. August 1945, war das malerisch um mehrere Höfe gruppierte Ensemble Schauplatz der Potsdamer Konferenz.

Séances apparently took place here, as did meetings of a secret society. Friedrich Wilhelm II, who followed his childless uncle Friedrich II onto the throne, created a type of counter Sanssouci here on the Sacred Lake. There are also vineyards and garden artistry, and a palace that was exquisitely furnished according to the style of the time. But where in Sanssouci the spirit of enlightenment blew on Friedrich's round table, his nephew surrounded himself with Freemasons and members of the Rosicrucian order, and wandered alone through the park lost in thoughts.

The Marble Palace which Carl von Gontard built him on the shore of the Sacred Lake was furnished by Carl Gotthard Langhans with the most beautiful early neo-classical interiors. At least as attractive is the surrounding New Garden, laid out in the style of a romantic landscape park. A Doric temple ruin sinks half into the ground on the shores of the lake – the building contains the kitchen of the palace and is connected to it with an underground hallway. An ice cellar in the shape of a pyramid is meant to symbolise an access to the underworld. A shell grotto served for the gatherings of the Freemason brothers. In the dairy the milk from the cows grazing in the park was processed, in the palm house of the orangery there were, and still are, concerts. And at the southern end of the park the tower-like Gothic library houses more than 1000 books.

After the death of Friedrich Wilhelm II the expansion of the Marble Palace came to a halt and was only completed by Friedrich Wilhelm IV, who had yet another pompous building, the Belvedere on the Pfingstberg, built. New life came to the New Garden with the crown prince Wilhelm. From 1905 the son of Kaiser Wilhelm II lived in the Marble Palace with his wife Cecilie until the adjacent Cecilienhof was completed in 1917. Here, in the last Hohenzollern palace, which Paul Schultze-Naumburg designed in the style of an English country house for the crown prince couple, the family lived until the end of the Second World War. Shortly after, from 17 July to 2 August 1945 the picturesque ensemble, which is grouped around various courtyards, was the setting for the Potsdam conference.

Um sich von Sanssouci abzusetzen, der Schöpfung seines Onkels Friedrich II., ließ sich dessen Nachfolger Friedrich Wilhelm II. am Ufer des Heiligen Sees eine neue zeitgemäße Sommerresidenz errichten. Das Marmorpalais entstand von 1787 bis 1792 nach Plänen von Carl von Gontard. Vom Belvedere auf dem Dach blickt man weit in die Havellandschaft. Die kostbaren Innenräume gestaltete Carl Gotthard Langhans, der Architekt des Brandenburger Tors in Berlin. Langhans erdachte auch die Schlossküche in Form eines halb in der Erde versunkenen antiken Tempels. Ein unterirdischer Gang verband sie mit dem Schloss.

In order to distance himself from Sanssouci, the creation of his uncle Friedrich II, his successor Friedrich Wilhelm II built a new modern summer residence on the shores of the Sacred Lake. The Marble Palace was built from 1787 to 1792 from plans by Carl von Gontard. From the Belvedere on the roof, you can see far into the Havelland region. The precious interiors were designed by Carl Gotthard Langhans, architect of the Brandenburg Gate in Berlin. Langhans also came up with the palace kitchen in the form of an ancient temple half sunk into the ground. An underground passageway connected it to the palace.

Nicht nur frühklassizistische Architekturmotive finden sich in dem nach Wörlitzer Vorbild gestalteten Neuen Garten, sondern auch damals hochaktuelle ägyptische Motive. Der Kopfbau der Orangerie wird durch eine Sphinx sowie ägyptische Götterfiguren aus der Werkstatt von Johann Gottfried Schadow bewacht. Neben den Pflanzenhallen beherbergt die Orangerie den holzvertäfelten Palmensaal, in dem damals wie heute festlich musiziert wird. Friedrich Wilhelm II. war ein begabter Cellospieler, der dort bei Konzerten auch vor Gästen auftrat.

The New Garden, designed in the style of the Wörlitz Park, offers not just early neo-classical architectural motifs but also Egyptian motifs, which were the height of fashion at the time. The front building of the Orangery is guarded by a sphinx and Egyptian deities from the workshop of Johann Gottfried Schadow. In addition to the Plant Hall, the Orangery is home to the wood-panelled Palm Hall, which then as now was used to hold concerts. Friedrich Wilhelm II was a talented cello player who also appeared in front of guests during concerts in the hall.

Das Holländische Etablissement liegt an der Hauptallee des Neuen Gartens in Sichtweite zum Seeufer. Im späten 18. Jahrhundert lebten hier Bedienstete des Königs und auch heute noch werden die Häuser und Wohnungen an Beschäftigte der Stiftung Preußische Schlösser und Gärten vermietet. Holländische Motive waren in der Potsdamer Architektur seit dem Bau des berühmten Holländischen Viertels in den 1730er Jahren überaus beliebt.

The Dutch Etablissement is situated on the main avenue of the New Garden within sight of the lake shore. In the late 18th century, servants of the king were housed here, and even today the houses and apartments are rented to employees of the Foundation for Prussian Palaces and Gardens Foundation. Dutch motifs were extremely popular in Potsdam architecture after the construction of the famous Dutch Quarter in the 1730s.

Friedrich Wilhelm II. war Freimaurer und hing als Mitglied der Rosenkreuzer esoterischen Ideen an. Parkbauten wie die Gotische Bibliothek und der Eiskeller in Form einer Pyramide sind nicht nur damals modische Zutaten sentimentaler Landschaftsparks, sondern spiegeln auch die Gedankenwelt des Königs wieder. Zu DDR-Zeiten war aus der Gotischen Bibliothek eine einsturzgefährdete Ruine geworden. Sie konnte nur gerettet werden, indem man die Außenmauern von 1995 bis 1997 Stein für Stein demontierte und nach der Sicherung der Fundamente an gleicher Stelle wieder in das neue Mauerwerk einfügte.

Friedrich Wilhelm II was a Freemason and, as a member of the Rosicrucians, had esoteric ideas. Park buildings such as the Gothic library and the ice house in the form of a pyramid are not only erstwhile fashionable ingredients of a sentimental landscape park, but also reflect the thoughts of the king. In the time of the GDR, the Gothic library became a ruin in danger of collapse. The only way to save it was by dismantling the outer walls stone by stone and, after securing the foundations, rebuilding the walls on the same site, a process which took place from 1995-97.

Als letzter Schlossbau der Hohenzollern entstand für Kronprinz Wilhelm und Kronprinzessin Cecilie von 1913 bis 1917 am nördlichen Rand des Neuen Gartens der Cecilienhof. Der Architekt Paul Schultze-Naumburg entwarf ein weitläufiges Gebäude im Stil englischer Landsitze – was während des Ersten Weltkriegs zu Kritik in der deutschen Presse führte. Das letzte Kronprinzenpaar des Deutschen Reichs lebte auch nach dem Ende der Monarchie im Cecilienhof. Nach ihrer Flucht tagte hier im Sommer 1945 die Potsdamer Konferenz. Sowjetische Soldaten pflanzten damals im Schlosshof einen Stern aus roten Blumen (S. 117).

Built from 1913-17 on the northern edge of the New Garden, the Cecilienhof was the last Hohenzollern palace, constructed for Crown Prince Wilhelm and Crown Princess Cecilie. Architect Paul Schultze-Naumburg designed a vast building in the style of an English country manor, which led to criticism in the German press during the First World War. The last Crown Prince and Princess of the German Empire lived on in the Cecilienhof even after the end of the monarchy. After their escape, the Potsdam conference was held here in the summer of 1945. On that occasion, Soviet soldiers planted a star made of red flowers in the courtyard (p. 117).

Seit der Wiedereröffnung 2001 genießen Besucher wieder „Potsdams schönste Aussicht" von den Doppeltürmen – wie einst Friedrich Wilhelm IV., nach dessen Ideen das Belvedere auf dem Pfingstberg entstand. Zu DDR-Zeiten war es jahrzehntelang vom Verfall bedroht, bis sich 1987 engagierte Bürger für den Erhalt und Wiederaufbau des vernachlässigten Bauwerks stark machten. Das Belvedere wurde so zu einem Symbol der friedlichen Revolution in Potsdam. Renoviert werden konnte es schließlich in den 1990er Jahren durch Millionenspenden von Werner Otto und Hermann-Hinrich Reemtsma.

Since its reopening in 2001, visitors can once again enjoy „Potsdam's most beautiful view" from the double towers, as once did Friedrich Wilhelm IV, who had the Belvedere on the Pfingstberg built according to his ideas. In the time of the GDR, it was threatened by decay for decades, until in 1987 city residents became involved in the preservation and rehabilitation of the neglected building. The Belvedere has in this way become a symbol of the peaceful revolution in Potsdam. It was finally restored in the 1990s thanks to a donation of millions from Werner Otto and Hermann-Hinrich Reemtsma.

Auch der nahe Pomonatempel war fast verschwunden – durch Vandalismus. 1990 gab es nur noch klägliche Reste des Tempelchens, das der 19jährige Karl Friedrich Schinkel als Erstlingswerk für einen preußischen Geheimrat entwarf. Wiederaufgebaut wurde es dank der Hermann Reemtsma Stiftung und der Freunde der Preußischen Schlösser und Gärten e.V.

The nearby Pomona temple was also nearly destroyed through vandalism. In 1990 there remained only pitiful remnants of this little temple, which was designed by the 19 year-old Karl Friedrich Schinkel as his first work for a Prussian Privy Councillor. It was rebuilt thanks to the Hermann Reemtsma Foundation and the Friends of the Prussian Palaces and Gardens Association.

6

Karl Friedrich Schinkel war auch beteiligt an der Uminterpretation original russischer Baupläne für die Alexander-Newski-Gedächtniskirche, die Teil der Kolonie Alexandrowka ist. Für zwölf Sänger eines russischen Soldatenchors errichtete man von 1826 bis 1829 Holzhäuser, die das Heimweh lindern halfen.

Karl Friedrich Schinkel was also involved in the reinterpretation of the original Russian blueprints for the Alexander Nevsky Memorial Church, which is part of the Alexandrovka colony. From 1826 to 1829, wooden houses were built for twelve members of a Russian soldier choir, which helped to alleviate their homesickness.

Rund um die Glienicker Brücke

England und Italien – selten stehen sie sich so nahe gegenüber. Zwar ließ sich Prinz Carl, der dritte Sohn Friedrich Wilhelms III., im Freundeskreis gern Sir Charles nennen – Schloss Glienicke, das er sich direkt an der Glienicker Brücke von Karl Friedrich Schinkel umbauen ließ, ist jedoch ein italienischer Traum in Reinkultur. Das schlichte Landhaus, das zuvor dem Staatskanzler Karl August von Hardenberg gehört hatte, wurde unter Schinkels Händen zur heiteren Villa. Prinz Carl, der prägende Eindrücke als Jugendlicher auf einer Italienreise empfangen hatte, sammelte antike Spolien und Statuen, die er in Haus und Garten verteilte. Inmitten der Parklandschaft von Peter Joseph Lenné entstand eine Fülle reizvoller Nebengebäude: die Große Neugierde, ein Aussichtspunkt mit Blick auf Potsdam und Havel, die intimere Kleine Neugierde, ein als Teehaus genutzter Gartenpavillon. Am Hochufer der Havel gestaltete Schinkel das Billardhaus zum Casino um und umgab es mit einer repräsentativen Pergola. Im ab 1850 errichteten Klosterhof kamen mittelalterliche und byzantinische Stücke der prinzlichen Sammlung unter. Und im benachbarten Ort Klein-Glienicke gestaltete der romantische Prinz eine ganze Siedlung aus Schweizerhäusern, legte alpine Schluchten am nahen Böttcherberg an. Der Weg nach Italien führte eben durch die Schweiz.

Ein ganz anderer Wind weht auf dem benachbarten Babelsberg. Hier ließ sich Carls älterer Bruder Wilhelm, der spätere Kaiser Wilhelm I., ein Schloss erbauen, und zwar im englischen Stil. Karl Friedrich Schinkel und sein Nachfolger Ludwig Persius entwarfen nach Vorgaben des Bauherrn ein neogotisches Cottage, das Schritt für Schritt erweitert wurde – um einen prächtigen oktogonalen Tanzsaal und einen Speisesaal im Tudorstil. Schloss Babelsberg, mit seiner Backsteinoptik, den Zinnen und Türmchen, ist ein romantisches Ritterschloss des 19. Jahrhunderts. Und auch hier ist es die umgebende Parklandschaft, die dem Schloss seinen Rahmen gibt: der weit über die Havel reichende Blick, Parkbauten wie das neogotische Matrosenhaus, das am Ufer der Havel gelegene Kleine Schloss und der als Ausguck dienende Flatowturm. Hermann Fürst von Pückler-Muskau, der die Parkgestaltung von Peter Joseph Lenné übernahm, verzweifelte zwar anfangs am sandigen Grund. Doch das am Havelufer im normannischen Burgenstil erbaute Dampfmaschinenhaus sorgte schließlich für ausreichende Bewässerung.

Zu Zeiten der deutschen Teilung durchschnitt die Mauer das Gartenreich, versperrte den Blick auf Havelseen und die Glienicker Brücke, wo zu Mauerzeiten russische gegen amerikanische Spione ausgetauscht worden sind. Heute ist das Parkreich wieder unzerteilt genießbar.

England and Italy – seldom do they stand so close to one another. Although Prince Carl, the third son of Friedrich Wilhelm III, liked to be called Sir Charles by his friends – Glienicke Palace, which Karl Friedrich Schinkel rebuilt directly at the Glienicke bridge, is an pure Italian dream. The simple country house, which formerly belonged to the Chancellor Karl August von Hardenberg, became a bright villa at the hands of Schinkel. Prince Carl, who received formative impressions on his travel to Italy as a youth, collected antique spolia and statues which he distributed throughout the house and garden. In the middle of the park by Peter Joseph Lenné there was a wealth of attractive outbuildings: The „Great Curiosity", a lookout point with a view over Potsdam and the Havel and the more intimate „Small Curiosity" which is a garden pavilion used as a tea house. On the banks of the Havel river Schinkel remodelled the billiard house into a casino, and surrounded it with a representative pergola. Into the cloister, which was built from 1850, came middle aged and Byzantine pieces from the princely collection. In the neighbouring Klein-Glienicke the romantic prince created an entire settlement of Swiss chalets and created Alpine gorges in the nearby Böttcherberg hill. The way to Italy led through Switzerland.

A completely different wind blew over the neighbouring Babelsberg hill. Here Carl's older brother Wilhelm, who was later Kaiser Wilhelm I, had a palace built in English style. Karl Friedrich Schinkel and his successor Ludwig Persius designed a neo-gothic cottage according to the specifications of the owner, and it was expanded step by step – with a magnificent octagonal ballroom and a dining room in Tudor style. Babelsberg Palace, with its brick appearance, the battlements and turrets, is a romantic knight's castle from the 19th century. Here too is the surrounding parkland which frames the palace: The view that reaches well past the Havel, park buildings such as the neo-gothic mariner's home, the Small Palace on the bank of the Havel and the Flatow tower that served as a lookout point. Hermann Fürst von Pückler-Muskau, who took over the park design from Peter Joseph Lenné, initially despaired at the sandy ground. However the steam engine house, in Norman building style, on the banks of the Havel River finally ensured adequate irrigation.

At the time of Germany's division the wall cut through the garden area, blocking the view of the Havel lakes and the Glienicke bridge where the Russian and American spies were exchanged. Today the park area can be enjoyed without the division.

Schloss und Park Glienicke an der Havel gehörten seit 1824 Prinz Carl von Preußen, dem jüngeren Bruder von Friedrich Wilhelm IV. und Wilhelm I. Prominent an der Straße von Berlin nach Potsdam nahe der Glienicker Brücke gelegen, hatte es hier schon seit Mitte des 18. Jahrhunderts ein adliges Gut gegeben, dessen letzter Vorbesitzern der preußische Staatskanzler Karl August Fürst von Hardenberg war. Bereits Hardenberg beauftragte Schinkel und Lenné mit der Umgestaltung von Gutshaus und Park – ein Team, das auch für Prinz Carl tätig blieb. Die Löwenfontäne entstand nach Schinkels Entwurf 1837/38.

From 1824, Glienecke Palace and Park on the Havel belonged to Prince Carl of Prussia, the younger brother of Friedrich Wilhelm IV and Wilhelm I. Prominently situated on the road from Berlin to Potsdam near the Glienicke Bridge, a nobleman's estate had existed here since the mid-18th century, the previous owner of which was the Prussian Chancellor Karl August Fürst von Hardenberg. Hardenberg commissioned Schinkel and Lenné to transform the manor house and park; a team that was also still working for Prince Carl. The lion fountain was built in 1837/38 according to Schinkel's sketches.

Das Glienicker Schloss ist das Resultat vieler Umbauten, die mit Schinkels Wirken längst nicht abgeschlossen waren. An seiner Westseite steht eine Kopie der Venus Italica von Antonio Canova. Der Kavalierflügel erhielt seine heutige Gestalt 1828 durch Schinkel und Ludwig Persius. Er beherbergte Wirtschaftsräume, den Pferdestall mit 24 Boxen, Wohnräume für Bedienstete sowie zwei Gästezimmer, in denen des Prinzen Adjutanten wohnten. Dem Turm, nach Schinkels Angaben von Persius ausgeführt, setzte man erst 1871/72 das spätklassizistische Obergeschoss mit dem markanten Säulen-Bogen-Motiv auf.

Glienicke Palace is the result of many alterations that were far from finished with Schinkel's work. On its west side is a copy of the Venus Italica by Antonio Canova. The Cavalier wing was given its present form in 1828 by Schinkel and Ludwig Persius. It contained commercial areas, stables with 24 stalls, and living space for staff, as well as two guest rooms where the prince's aides lived. The tower was built by Persius according to Schinkel's plans. The late neo-classical upper floor, with its distinctive pillar arch motif, was only drawn up in 1871/72.

◄
Schinkels Meisterschüler Ludwig Persius entwarf 1840 das Stibadium als halbrunden überdachten Teeplatz, von dem man seinerzeit eine atemberaubende Aussicht über die Havel nach Potsdam genießen konnte. Das hölzerne Dach wird durch die Marmorkopie der Felicitas Publica (Öffentliches Wohl) von Christian Daniel Rauch getragen.

Schinkel's master student, Ludwig Persius, designed the Stibadium in 1840 as a semi-circular covered tea house, which at that time offered breathtaking views over the Havel towards Potsdam. The wooden roof was supported by a marble copy of Felicitas Publica (Public Welfare) by Christian Daniel Rauch.

◄◄
Schinkels Einstand für den Prinzen Carl in Glienicke war der Umbau des alten Billardhauses in das Casino, ein von Pergolen gesäumtes Gartengebäude oberhalb des Havelufers. Vielen gilt es als perfekte Verkörperung des preußischen Arkadiens.

Schinkel's first Glienicke commission for Prince Carl was the conversion of the old billiard hall into the casino, a garden building flanked by pergolas on the banks of the Havel. Many consider it the perfect embodiment of Prussian Arcadia.

▶
Ebenfalls dem Sehen und Gesehenwerden diente die Große Neugierde, ein Rundpavillon in Gestalt des Athener Lysikrates-Monuments. Im Sommer 1835 mit einer Teegesellschaft eingeweiht, konnten die hohen Herrschaften den Verkehr auf der neuen Glienicker Brücke verfolgen.

Serving the important end of seeing and being seen was the „Great Curiosity", a round pavilion in the shape of the Athens Lysikrates monument. Inaugurated with a tea party in the summer of 1835, from here high-ranking lords and ladies were able to watch the traffic over the new Glienicke Bridge.

Keins der Potsdamer Schlösser dürfte auf so vielfältige Verwendungen zurückblicken wie das Jagdschloss Glienicke, dieses 300 Jahre alte Schmuckstück unweit der Glienicker Brücke: Jagdschloss, Lazarett, Tapetenfabrik, Waisenhaus und wieder Jagdschloss, dann Residenz des Berliner NS-Oberbürgermeisters Lippert, nach dem Krieg Jugendherberge und Filmkulisse. Die deutsche Teilung brachte das im südwestlichsten Zipfel West-Berlins gelegene Jagdschloss in eine ungünstige Lage, eingeklemmt zwischen der als „Blinddarm der DDR" bezeichneten Sondersicherheitszone Klein-Glienicke und dem Glienicker See. Der Haupteingang musste auf die Rückseite verlegt werden, weil die Zufahrtsstraße jenseits des Eisernen Vorhangs gelandet war. Heute wird es für Tagungen und Seminare genutzt.

None of Potsdam's castles have seen quite as many different uses as Jagdschloss Glienicke, this 300-year-old gem close to Glienicker Bridge: hunting lodge, military hospital, wallpaper factory, orphanage and back to hunting lodge, before becoming the residence of Berlin's National Socialist mayor, Lippert, and then a youth hostel and film backdrop after the war. The partition of Germany put the hunting lodge, located at the most south-westerly point of West Berlin, in an unfavourable position, sandwiched between the Klein-Glienicke special security zone described as an „appendix of the GDR" and the Glienicker See lake. The main entrance had to be moved to the rear because the access road now lay behind the Iron Curtain. Today, it is used for conferences and seminars.

Potsdam und die Glienicker Brücke fest im Blick, ließ sich Prinz Wilhelm, später als preußischer König und erster deutscher Kaiser Wilhelm I. bekannt, ebenfalls ein Sommerschloss errichten. Schloss Babelsberg, nach Plänen von Schinkel 1833 begonnen und bis 1849 mehrfach erweitert, kopiert die Stilformen englischer Tudorgotik. Wilhelms Gemahlin Augusta, eine Prinzessin von Sachsen-Weimar, war begeisterte Englandliebhaberin und Anhängerin der damals hochmodernen Neogotik. Sie engagierte auch den berühmten Gartengestalter Fürst Hermann von Pückler-Muskau.

With Potsdam and the Glienicke Bridge firmly in view, Prince Wilhelm, later known as the King of Prussia and the first German Kaiser Wilhelm I, also added a summer palace. Babelsberg Palace, begun in 1833 according to plans by Schinkel and expanded many times until 1849, echoed the English Tudor Gothic style. Wilhelm's wife Augusta, a Saxe-Weimar princess, was an enthusiastic lover of England and a supporter of the then ultra-modern neo-Gothic style. She also hired the famous landscape designer Fürst Hermann von Pückler-Muskau.

Immer wieder wurde Schloss Babelsberg zum Schauplatz deutscher Geschichte. Auf der Schlossterrasse fand 1862 das entscheidende Gespräch statt, das zur Ernennung Bismarcks zum preußischen Ministerpräsidenten führte. Seit 1961 durchschnitt die Berliner Mauer den sanft zur Havel abfallenden Pleasureground direkt vor dem Schloss. 28 Jahre lang lag das 1843 von Ludwig Persius entworfene Dampfmaschinenhaus mit seinem als Turm getarnten Schornstein im Todesstreifen und war nur für DDR-Grenzer erreichbar.

Babelsberg Palace has repeatedly been the location for developments in German history. In 1862, the decisive meeting which led to the appointment of Bismarck as Prussian Prime Minister took place on the palace terrace. From 1961, the Berlin Wall cut through the pleasure park in front of the palace which slopes gently down to the Havel. For 28 years, the steam engine house designed by Ludwig Persius in 1843, with its chimney disguised as a tower, lay in the no-man's-land between East and West and was accessible only to the East-German wards of the frontier.

Zu den neogotischen Babelsberger Parkbauten gehört die Gerichtslaube – mit der Besonderheit, dass sie in Teilen sogar echt gotisch ist. Als man in Berlin in den 1860er Jahren das Rathaus aus dem 13. Jahrhundert für den Neubau des Roten Rathauses abriss, blieb die originale Gerichtslaube zunächst stehen. Doch da viele Berliner ihre Notdurft darin verrichteten, wurde der funktionslos gewordene und als Geruchslaube diffamierte Bau zum öffentlichen Ärgernis. Die Stadt Berlin schenkte das Baumaterial schließlich dem Kaiser, der die „Geruchslaube" 1871 in Babelsberg wieder aufbauen ließ.

The Babelsberg neo-Gothic park buildings include the Court Arbour, notable for the fact that parts of it really are gothic. When the 13th century town hall was demolished in 1860s Berlin to make way for the construction of the Red Town Hall, the original Court Arbour initially remained standing. But as many Berliners used it to relieve themselves in, it fell out of use and became infamous only for its stench. The city of Berlin eventually made a gift of building materials to the Kaiser, who in 1871 commissioned the rebuilding of the Court Arbour in Babelsberg.

▶
Die 67 Hektar große Pfaueninsel ist ein magischer Ort, auch wenn die Überfahrt mit der Fähre nur Minuten dauert. Ungestörte Stunden mit seiner Geliebten, der Gräfin Lichtenau, hatte Friedrich Wilhelm II. im Sinn, als er den Potsdamer Hofzimmermeister Johann Gottlieb Brendel mit dem Bau des hölzernen Schlösschens im Stil einer romantischen Ruine beauftragte.

The 67-hectare Pfaueninsel, or "Peacock Island" is a magical place, although the ferry crossing takes mere minutes. When he commissioned the Potsdam court's master carpenter Johann Gottlieb Brendel to build a miniature wooden castle in the style of a romantic ruin, Friedrich Wilhelm II was imagining undisturbed hours with his mistress, the Countess Lichtenau.

◀
Für dessen Sohn Friedrich Wilhelm III. erweiterte Schinkel ein älteres Kavalierhaus. Der König hatte in Danzig ein vom Abriss bedrohtes gotisches Patrizierhaus gekauft, ließ es Stein für Stein abtragen und in einen Anbau einfügen.

For his son, Friedrich Wilhelm III, Schinkel expanded a former gentleman's house. The king had bought a Gothic mansion in Gdansk which was threatened with demolition. He brought it stone by stone to the island and had it built into an extension.

Ihr Architekt Ludwig Persius wollte sie schlicht „das Schiff" nennen. Die 1844 errichtete Heilandskirche am Port von Sacrow steht einige hundert Meter vom Dorf Sacrow entfernt am Ufer des Jungfernsees. König Friedrich Wilhelm IV. wünschte sich an dieser exponierten Stelle einen Kirchenbau in frühchristlich-italienischer Gestalt mit freistehendem Glockenturm. Nach dem Mauerbau 1961 stand die Kirche zwar noch auf DDR-Gebiet, doch jenseits von Todesstreifen und Sperrmauer und war damit für die Gemeinde unerreichbar geworden. Der erste Gottesdienst nach 28 Jahren wurde am Heiligabend 1989 gefeiert.

Its architect Ludwig Persius wanted simply to call it „the ship". The Church of the Redeemer, built in 1844 in the port of Sacrow, lies a few hundred metres from the village on the shores of the Jungfernsee. In this exposed spot, King Friedrich Wilhelm IV wanted to build a church in the early Italian Christian style with a freestanding bell tower. After the Wall went up in 1961, the church was in GDR territory, but as it lay beyond no-man's-land and the outer wall, it became inaccessible to the community. The first service for 28 years was celebrated in 1989 on Christmas Eve.

Die Stadt Potsdam

Die Stadt hat ihr Herz verloren – und viele haben ihr Herz an sie verloren. Die brandenburgische Landeshauptstadt, dreißig Kilometer von der West-Berliner City entfernt, gilt als die feinere kleine Schwester der Bundeshauptstadt und ist ein bevorzugter Wohnort wohlhabender Berliner. Die von Ludwig Persius und anderen erbauten klassizistischen Villen erstrahlen wieder im freundlichen Gelb, die Berliner Vorstadt am Heiligen See oder die gründerzeitliche Brandenburger Vorstadt sind beliebte Wohnviertel. Potsdam ist mit Universität, Fachhochschule, Forschungseinrichtungen und Einstein-Forum ein bedeutender Standort der Wissenschaft, das 2006 im neuen Haus wiedereröffnete Hans-Otto-Theater und der Nikolaisaal bieten in moderner Architektur hochrangige Kulturevents, und auch die Filmstudios in Babelsberg, die 2012 ihr hundertstes Jubiläum feiern, verzeichnen dank internationaler Großproduktionen wieder Erfolge.

Die malerischen Gassen des unter König Friedrich Wilhelm I. angelegten Holländischen Viertels und die geschäftigen Einkaufsstraßen der barocken Stadterweiterung rund um die Brandenburger Straße lassen fast vergessen, dass der eigentliche Potsdamer Stadtkern Opfer des Bombenhagels im Zweiten Weltkrieg und der anschließenden Abrisswut der DDR wurde. Geblieben ist vom ursprünglichen Potsdam das Karree rund um den Neuen Markt, mit Ratswaage, königlichem Kutschstall, heute Haus der Brandenburgisch-Preußischen Geschichte, und der ehemalige Marstall, heute als Filmmuseum genutzt. Gegenüber am Alten Markt haben Nikolaikirche und Altes Ratshaus die Zerstörung überlebt. Doch der Kern der Innenstadt, das Stadtschloss, das vom 17. Jahrhundert bis 1918 Residenz der Kurfürsten und Könige war, wurde 1959 und 1960 auf Anordnung Walter Ulbrichts gesprengt. Ein in den historischen Formen und mit den barocken Fassaden versehener Neubau, der künftig den Landtag beherbergen soll, ist derzeit in Bau, geplant wird auch die Rekonstruktion der geschichtsträchtigen Garnisonkirche. Die Sehnsucht nach Vergangenheit ist mächtig in Potsdam – wer sich in der Stadt bewegt, kann sich ihr nicht verschließen.

The city lost its heart – and many have lost their heart to it. The Brandenburg state capital, thirty kilometres from the city of West Berlin, is the beautiful smaller sister of the nation's capital and is a popular residence of wealthy Berliners. The classical villas built by Ludwig Persius and others are once again shining in friendly yellow, the Berlin suburb on the Sacred Lake or the early Brandenburg suburbs are popular residential areas. With universities, universities of applied sciences, research institutes and the Einstein Forum, Potsdam is an important location for science, which offers high calibre cultural events in modern architecture in the new building of the reopened (2006) Hans Otto Theatre and the Nikolai Hall, and also the film studios on Babelsberg which have celebrated their 100th anniversary in 2012 and, thanks to large international productions, are once again recording success.

The picturesque alleys in the Dutch quarter, which was laid out by King Friedrich Wilhelm I, and the busy shopping streets of the Baroque city expansion around Brandenburger Straße almost let you forget that the Potsdam city centre fell victim to a hail of bombs in the Second World War and the subsequent demolition frenzy of the GDR. What remains of the original Potsdam is the square around the New Market with the old weighing house, king's coach house which is today the house of Brandenburg-Prussian history and the former stables which are today used as a film museum. Opposite the Old Market the Nikolai church and the old courthouse survived the destruction. But the core of the inner city, the City Palace, which was the residence of electors and kings from the 17th century until 1918, was blown up in 1959 and 1960 on the orders of Walter Ulbricht. A new construction in the historical form and with Baroque façades, which in future is planned to house the state parliament, is currently being built, and the rebuilding of the historical Garrison Church is also planned. The desire for history is powerful in Potsdam – anyone who visits the city can't avoid it.

Trotz immenser Verluste infolge der Bombardierung der Stadt im April 1945 und durch Abrisse zu DDR-Zeiten wird die Potsdamer Innenstadt noch immer durch bedeutende Bauten des 18. Jahrhunderts geprägt. Zu ihnen gehören die Alte Wache, 1795 bis 1797 nach Plänen von Andreas Ludwig Krüger als Zoll- und Wachgebäude entstanden, sowie das Haus „Im Güldenen Arm", eines der wenigen gut erhaltenen Fachwerk-Bürgerhäuser der 1730er Jahre. Geschlossene Straßenbilder haben sich im Holländischen Viertel (S. 160) und in der Wilhelm-Staab-Straße (S. 161) erhalten.

Despite immense losses as a result of the bombing of the city in April 1945 and demolitions in the time of the GDR, the centre of Potsdam is today still characterised by important buildings from the 18th century. They include the Old Guard, built from 1795 to 1797 as a customs and guard house according to plans developed by Andreas Ludwig Krüger, and the house "Im Güldenen Arm" ("The Gilded Arm"), one of the few well-preserved half-timbered town houses of the 1730s. Images of the enclosed streets have been preserved in the Dutch Quarter (p. 160) and Wilhelm-Staab-Straße (p. 161).

HAAR
Museumsshop

P LF 28

Eine Besonderheit der Potsdamer Stadtbaukunst ist das Holländische Viertel, von 1733 bis 1740 im Rahmen der Zweiten Barocken Stadterweiterung nach Ideen des holländischen Baumeisters Jan Bouman (Johann Baumann) errichtet. Es sollte niederländische Einwanderer nach Potsdam locken, was nur teilweise gelang. Die 134 Typenbauten aus rotem Ziegelstein stehen entweder mit ihren Giebel zur Straße oder aber mit der Längsseite. Um 1780 ließ Friedrich II. die holländische Architekturmode noch einmal aufgreifen und am Bassin repräsentative dreigeschossige Bürgerhäuser bauen.

A special feature of the Potsdam city architecture is the Dutch Quarter, built from 1733 to 1740 as part of the Second Baroque city expansion according to the ideas of Dutch architect Jan Bouman (Johann Baumann). It was intended to attract Dutch immigrants to Potsdam, but was only partially successful. The 134 red brick buildings were constructed with either the gable or the long side facing the street. In 1780 Friedrich II again requested the Dutch architectural style and commissioned the building of prestigious three-storey town houses on Bassin.

KIND
HÖRGERÄTE

* Café Heider *
Caféhaustradition
seit 1878
* Café Heider *

Ein weiteres „holländisches" Element der Stadtgestaltung war der in der Art einer Gracht angelegte Stadtkanal, den man in den 1960er Jahren zugeschüttet hat. Seit einigen Jahren wird er abschnittsweise wieder freigelegt und als innerstädtische Promenade genutzt. Im 18. Jahrhundert war Potsdam von einer Zoll- und Akzisemauer umgeben, die auch das Desertieren der Soldaten verhindern sollte. Erhalten haben sich einige der Stadttore, so das Nauener Tor (S. 164-165), das Jägertor (links) und das Brandenburger Tor (S. 168-169).

A further "Dutch" element of urban design was introduced in the form of a city canal, which was filled in the 1960s. For several years it has once again been partially exposed, and is used as urban promenade. In the 18th century Potsdam was surrounded by a customs and excise wall, which was also intended to prevent the desertion of soldiers. Some of the city gates have survived: the Nauen Gate (p. 164-165), the Hunter's Gate (left) and the Brandenburg Gate (p. 168-169) .

MDCCLX

Mitte des 19. Jahrhunderts zog die Dampfkraft in Potsdam ein – zunächst mit dem Ziel, die Fontänen von Sanssouci zum Sprudeln zu bringen. An der Neustädter Havelbucht entstand 1841 bis 1843 unter der Leitung von Ludwig Persius ein Dampfmaschinenhaus in der Gestalt einer orientalischen Moschee. Eine 82 PS starke Dampfmaschine von August Borsig pumpte das Havelwasser bis auf den Ruinenberg (S. 24), von wo es mittels Schwerkraft die Fontänen des Schlossparks speiste.

In the mid-19th century, steam power came to Potsdam, initially with the aim of making the fountains of Sanssouci bubble. Under the direction of Ludwig Persius, from 1841 – 43 a steam engine house was constructed at Neustädter shore of the Havel river in the shape of an oriental mosque. A 82-horsepower steam engine by August Borsig pumped water up the Havel as far as the Ruinenberg (p. 24), where it fed the fountains of the park using the forces of gravity.

Der Einsteinturm des Architekten Erich Mendelsohn hat Architekturgeschichte geschrieben. In dem von 1919 bis 1924 gebauten Sonnenobservatorium auf dem Potsdamer Telegrafenberg, das ein Turmteleskop enthält, sollte Albert Einsteins Allgemeine Relativitätstheorie experimentell bestätigt werden. Eigentlich wollte Mendelsohn das Gebäude vollständig aus Beton errichten lassen. In Vorbereitung der von 1997 bis 1999 erfolgten gründlichen Sanierung musste man jedoch feststellen, dass weite Teile der kühnen Schwünge und Rundungen in konventioneller Mauerwerkstechnik ausgeführt worden waren.

The Einstein Tower by architect Erich Mendelsohn wrote architectural history. In the solar observatory, which was built on the Telegrafenberg in Potsdam from 1919 to 1924 and contained a tower telescope, Albert Einstein's general theory of relativity was to be confirmed experimentally. Initially Mendelsohn wanted to make the building completely of concrete. In preparation for the renovation work which was carried out from 1997 to 1999, it was discovered that many of the daring turns and curves were completed using conventional masonry techniques.

Die Potsdamer Innenstadt umgibt ein Kranz von Vorstädten, in denen sich im 19. Jahrhundert Hofbedienstete, Offiziere und höhere Beamte in repräsentativen Villen ansiedelten. Nach dem Vorbild von Schinkels Römischen Bädern (S. 82–86) kreierten Architekten wie Persius und Hesse einen eigenen Potsdamer Villenstil.

The Potsdam city centre is surrounded by a ring of suburbs, where 19th century court servants, officers and senior officials lived in prestigious villas. Following the example of Schinkel's Roman Baths (pp. 82–86) architects such as Persius and Hesse created their own Potsdam villa style.

◀◀
Ein Musterbeispiel dieser italienisch anmutenden Turmvillen ist die Villa Schöningen an der Glienicker Brücke, 1843 von Persius für den Hofmarschall des Prinzen Carl entworfen. Heute betreibt Matthias Döpfner hier ein Privatmuseum, das auch an die Nutzung der Villa als DDR-Kinderheim erinnert.

A prime example of this Italianate style of turreted villa is the Villa Schöningen near the Glienicke Bridge, designed in 1843 by Persius for Prince Carl's Lord Chamberlain. Today, Matthias Döpfner runs a private museum here, which also recalls the use of the villa as a GDR orphanage.

◀◀
Im 17. Jahrhundert als Orangerie gebaut, beherbergte der Marstall des Stadtschlosses ab 1714 königliche Reitpferde. Seine jetzige Gestalt mit den Rossebändigern von Friedrich Christian Glume erhielt das Bauwerk 1746. 1981 eröffnete in dem von polnischen Handwerkern restaurierten Marstall das Filmmuseum. Im Hintergrund rechts ist die Baugrube für das neue Stadtschloss (S. 186-187) zu erkennen.

Built in the 17th century as an orangery, from 1714 onwards the stables of the City Palace accommodated royal horses. The building took on its present form, with Friedrich Christian Glume's horse-tamers, in 1746. The Film Museum opened in 1981 in the restored stables rebuilt by Polish artisans. In the background on the right, the excavations for the new City Palace (p. 186-187) can be seen.

◀
Auf der Rückseite des Marstalls steht ein Nachguss des Denkmals für Friedrich Wilhelm von Steuben, preußischer Offizier und Organisator der amerikanischen Revolutionsarmee, das der amerikanische Kongress 1911 Kaiser Wilhelm II. geschenkt hatte.

At the back of the stables stands a reproduction of the monument to Friedrich Wilhelm von Steuben, a Prussian officer and organiser of the American Revolutionary Army, which the U.S. Congress gifted to Kaiser Wilhelm II in 1911.

WAAGE

Potsdams intimster Stadtplatz ist der Neue Markt mit der Ratswaage. Im Hintergrund steht der Kutschpferdestall des Stadtschlosses, von 1787 bis 1790 nach Plänen von Andreas Ludwig Krüger entstanden. Zu DDR-Zeiten lagerte man dort Gemüse und Speisekartoffeln. Heute beherbergt der restaurierte Kutschpferdestall das Haus der Brandenburgisch-Preußischen Geschichte. Sein Mittelportal schmückt eine Quadriga, die von Friedrichs II. Leibkutscher Pfundt gelenkt wird.

Potsdam's most intimate town square is the New Market, where you will find the scale of the City Council. In the background is the stables of the City Palace coach horses, built from 1787-90 according to plans developed by Andreas Ludwig Krüger. In the time of the GDR, vegetables were stored here. Today, the restored stable is home to the House of Brandenburg-Prussian History. Its central entrance is embellished with a quadriga, driven by Friedrich II's coachman Pfundt.

◀◀

Potsdams zentraler Stadtplatz ist noch immer der Alte Markt – auch wenn er bei der alliierten Bombardierung vom April 1945 besonders stark zerstört wurde. Noch immer wirken die bereits in den 1960er bis 1980er Jahren wieder aufgebauten Baudenkmale etwas verloren. Erst durch den Wiederaufbau des Stadtschlosses (S. 186-187) und weiterer Leitbauten wird sich das Bild des historischen Platzes wieder runden. Das Alte Rathaus mit der vergoldeten Atlasfigur und das angrenzende sogenannte Knobelsdorffhaus konnten bereits 1966 als Kulturhaus wiedereröffnet werden.

Potsdam's central town square is still the Old Market, even after it was destroyed during the Allied bombing of April 1945. Rebuilt from the 1960s to the 1980s, the square's buildings still act as a monument to what was lost. Through the reconstruction of the City Palace (p. 186-187) and other landmark buildings, the image of the historic square is once more complete. The Old Town Hall with its gilded figure of Atlas and the adjoining so-called Knobelsdorff House were re-opened as a cultural centre as early as 1966.

◀

Den Anstoß zum Wiederaufbau des 1959 / 60 gesprengten Stadtschlosses gab der in Potsdam lebende Günther Jauch. Gemeinsam mit anderen Mäzenen brachte er das Geld auf, um das um 1700 errichtete Fortunaportal des Schlosses rekonstruieren zu konnen. 2002 wurde die originalgetreue Kopie des Portals einer staunenden Öffentlichkeit übergeben. Inzwischen ist die gesamte Fassade des Schlosses am Alten Markt wiederhergestellt.

The impetus for the reconstruction of the City Palace, blown up in 1959/60, came from Potsdam resident Günther Jauch. Together with other patrons, he raised the money to reconstruct the palace's Fortuna entrance, first built in 1700. In 2002, a faithful reproduction was delivered to an astonished public. By now the entire façade of the palace in the Old Market has been restored.

◀◀
Das 1772 fertiggestellte Palais Barberini bildet den südlichen Abschluss des Alten Marktes. Wer den namengebenden Palazzo in Rom kennt, dem wird die Ähnlichkeit sofort ins Auge springen, und dennoch trennen fast 140 Jahre die beiden Gebäude – wenn man es ganz genau nimmt, sogar doppelt so viele, denn der unter Friedrich dem Großen errichtete Bau fiel kurz vor Kriegsende noch den alliierten Bombern zum Opfer.

The Barberini Palace was completed in 1772, forming the southern boundary of the old market square. Anyone who is familiar with its namesake Palazzo Barberini in Rome will immediately notice the similarity even though the two buildings were constructed almost 140 years apart – or strictly speaking, twice that, because the building constructed by Frederick the Great fell victim to allied bombing shortly before the end of the war.

◀▶
Eine Kirche steht an dieser Stelle schon seit dem 13. Jahrhundert, als am Alten Markt die erste Pfarrkirche Potsdams entstand. Was Romanik, Gotik und Renaissance hinterlassen hatten, wurde vom Soldatenkönig abgerissen und durch einen nüchternen Neubau ersetzt, den sein Sohn Friedrich (der Große) mit einer übertriebenen Barockfassade versah. Nachdem die Kirche 1795 abgebrannt war, passierte drei Jahrzehnte lang gar nichts (es waren kriegerische Zeiten), bis 1837 endlich ein streng klassizistischer Neubau fertiggestellt werden konnte, der 1850 um die Kuppel ergänzt wurde.

A church has stood on this site since the 13th century, when Potsdam's first parish church was built in the old market square. The Soldier King demolished what was left of the Romanesque, Gothic and Renaissance eras and replaced it with an austere new building that was given an overstated Baroque facade by his son, Frederick (the Great). After the church burned down in 1795, nothing happened for three decades (these were times of war) until a severe neoclassical building was finally completed in 1837, to which a dome was added in 1850.

Zukunft durch Vergangenheit? Wo sich einst das Stadtschloss der brandenburgischen Kurfürsten und preußischen Könige erhob, wurde seit Februar 2011 ein Neubau für den Landtag von Brandenburg in Gestalt des Hohenzollernschlosses errichtet. Jahrelange Diskussionen über die Zukunft des Stadtzentrums waren vorausgegangen.

Future via the past? Where the City Palace of the electors of Brandenburg and the Prussian kings once stood, from February 2011 a new building has been built in the shape of the Hohenzollern palace which houses the Brandenburg state parliament. This decision was preceded by years of discussions about the future of the city centre.

Dank einer Millionenspende des bekennenden Potsdam-Fans Hasso Plattner kann das Gebäude mit Kopien der Knobelsdorffschen Fassaden versehen werden. Der historisierende Wiederaufbau des Landtags-Schlosses gilt als Weichenstellung für die Gestaltung der baulich disparaten Stadtmitte rund um den Alten Markt.

Thanks to a donation of millions from avowed Potsdam fan Hasso Plattner, the building will be provided with reproductions of Knobelsdorff's façades. The historicist reconstruction of the State Parliament Palace has served to set the design agenda for the structurally disparate city centre surrounding the Old Market.